LOVE IS THE GREATEST

I Corinthians 13

By

David Hocking

Hope for Today Publications   Tustin, California 92781

Love is the Greatest

ISBN 9780988243149

Printed in the United States of America

Copyright in 2014, HFT Publications

Tustin, California 92781

Library of Congress Cataloging-in-Publication Data.

Hocking, David

Table of Contents

Part One

The Definition of Love

Chapter One

The Definition of Love

What Is Love?

The desire to love and be loved is a fundamental part of human personality and need. It affects how we think, feel and relate to everything and everyone in life. It brings joy and great feelings of exhilaration but also causes enormous pain and hurt. At times, we feel overwhelmed by love's presence and at other times, we feel lonely and empty by its absence. It comforts us when nothing else will and unravels us when we least expect it. It makes us feel secure at times while at other times, it produces great insecurity and fear.

To some people, love is merely an emotion, a feeling that excites, warms, charms, encourages and strengthens us. It can be created by the fantasies of our mind or by the unexplained circumstances of our lives. It can be sentimental, sympathetic, understanding and kind or it can be threatening, jealous, suspicious and frightened.

Many people see love mostly as a physical attraction, a desire for physical intimacy or sexual expression. The term "make love" is used for physical involvement, yet sexual activity is often abusive, selfish and empty of loving feelings and verbal exchange that touches the heart. Sexual acts are often aggressive and hostile behavior, described more by lust and self-gratification than by loving response.

Love can cause emotional confusion and mental stress. It fluctuates in its impact upon us as we try to analyze and understand its effects. We can express its influence by helping others or by giving words of kindness and encouragement. We find it necessary to tell others of love's existence even when we are unsure of its nature and presence within us.

We can be deceived into believing that love exists in relationship to another person, only to discover that the other person is not affected in the same way. When we express love's presence and influence to others but it is not received well, we immediately feel hurt, rejected or angry. Our self esteem is threatened by an unresponsive person. Love can be quickly blended with pride, producing a resistant arrogance beneath the surface of our emotional state and making it difficult for us to be loving toward those who do not feel as we do. We feel attacked, and sometimes we seek revenge.

The Greek Language of Love

The ancient Greek and Roman world was filled with words of love. Among the philosophical systems that arose, there seemed to be an intense desire to understand and experience love. Great discussions of love are found in these writings, and much of it is intertwined with religious ideas and beliefs. The gods of the ancient Greeks were human in attribute and action and seemed to reflect the relationships and quest for love which were so prevalent in society at that time. Sexuality was prominent in these discussions and society at the time seemed to be exploring all avenues and methods of experiencing and expressing love.

Four major words were used in the *koine* (common) Greek of ancient times for love, but only three of these appear in the Bible:

Storge – family love

Phile – friendship love

Agape – spiritual love

Eros – sexual love (not used in the Bible)

The word "love" in English is used to describe all four of these Greek words. Our love can be expressed toward people and toward things. It can apply to a casual relationship or one that is more intimate. It can be shared with a stranger or with a friend whom we have known over the years. It can produce a variety of responses and responsibilities. It can be expressed in words and in deeds. It can be understood or misinterpreted. It can be received or rejected.

In order to gain a proper understanding of the depth and dimensions of love, let's start by seeing what the ancient Greeks and Romans thought about its differences and distinctions.

Sexual Love

While the word *eros* does not appear in the Bible, sexual love is described in some detail in Scripture. The Song of Solomon, the best of over one thousand songs written by King Solomon, is a romantic and erotic love poem to his one and only. The sensuality of this book of the Bible is unequaled in all of literature. It is romantic love at its best. It is sexual love as it was meant to be. It is filled with verbal enticement as well as strong words of commitment and loyalty. The actions of Solomon and his bride reveal that sexual pleasure is not only approved by the God of the Bible, but is actually encouraged.

Humans were designed as sexual creatures, though the reproductive processes of both animals and humans do not tell the story of sexual love. Love is not merely an act of physical anatomy and need that produces offspring; it becomes (in humans) a fundamental expression of personality and emotional oneness. It can bond, blend and build intimacy.

Sexual love brings relief, satisfaction, pleasure and closeness. It can also become destructive and abusive and can cause feelings of emptiness, loneliness and lack of fulfillment. It can be experienced without commitment, trust or respect, thereby becoming the most dangerous and deceiving form of love.

Sexual love can be stimulated by sight, sound, smell, taste or touch. A person can desire sexual involvement without knowing or caring about the person desired. Sexual desire can exist even when there is no external stimulation; it can be created in one's own mind.

Jesus Christ spoke of how a person can experience lust in the heart and, simply by looking, can desire sexual involvement:

> *I say to you that whoever looks at a woman to lust after her has already committed adultery with her in his heart* (Matthew 5:28).

The word "looks" denotes a continual habit. The word "woman" is singular, not plural. It is concentration on a particular woman with a specific intent – to commit adultery. The woman is married to another man and Jesus is condemning the mental thought of sexual intercourse with somebody else's wife. The sin lies in the desire to violate God's command, *"You shall not commit adultery"* (Exodus 20:14)

The Bible recognizes the tremendous pressure of sexual desire. The apostle Paul wrote this *to "the unmarried and to the widows"*

> *It is good for them if they remain even as I am; but if they cannot exercise self-control, let them marry. For it is better to marry than to burn with passion* (I Corinthians 7:8,9).

Later in the same chapter, he addressed those who had never married or experienced sexual intercourse (*"virgins"* v.25). The words "the unmarried" refer to those who were once married, but now because of divorce are single again. The word "widows" refers to those whose spouses had died. Having experienced sexual love and continuing sexual pressure ("burn with passion"), they were urged to get married rather than to become involved in sexual sin. The entire passage is dealing with how to avoid sexual immorality (cf. I Corinthians 7:2).

Sexual love is often stimulated by touch. I Corinthians 7:1 says, "*It is good for a man not to touch a woman.*" The issue is not a handshake, a brief hug or a kiss on the cheek in greeting someone. As is clear from verse 2, the issue involves sexual immorality – touching that solicits and stimulates a sexual response.

Sexual love needs to be the result of stronger love that is rooted in commitment, loyalty, trust and mutual respect. It is clear in the Bible that sexual love exists but should not culminate in sexual intercourse except within the bonds of holy matrimony.

Marriage is honorable among all, and the bed
undefiled; but fornicators and adulterers God
will judge (Hebrews 13:4).

Sexual sin is listed frequently in the Bible among the
lists of sins that reflect an unbelieving heart (I Corinthians
6:9; Galatians 5:19-21; Ephesians 5:3-5; Colossians 3:5-7;
I Peter 4:3; II Peter 2:18-22; Revelation 2:21-22; 9:21;
22:15) and includes the prospect of God's judgment.

Jesus also indicated that sexual sin is found in the
depravity of our own hearts (Mark 7:21-23). Sexual desire
can be so powerful that we are tempted to disobey God's
commands about how it is to be satisfied and fulfilled.

Once sexual intercourse takes place outside of
marriage, a person often tries to convince himself that he
(or she) is "in love". While sexual love is intense, it does not
result in marital love, the love of strong commitment and
fidelity. Marital love can be developed but sexual intimacy
before marriage confuses the issue and leads to self-
deception and inadequate conclusions about the nature and
expressions of love.

We all need to face the sobering reality that sexual
desire, attraction and involvement do not necessarily
indicate other kinds of love. God places sexual desire within

us and tells us how it should be controlled. He created sex and He knows how we can best experience fulfillment and lasting happiness through sex. In addition to problems of sexual disease and possible pregnancy, many people are deeply hurt emotionally because of sexual activity outside of marriage. I Peter 2:11 speaks of *"fleshly lusts that wage war against the soul."*

Sexual love that is not governed by friendship and spiritual love will soon deteriorate in its desirability and sense of satisfaction. Intimate relationships that continue over lengthy periods of time (outside marriage) are usually based on deeper ties and loyalties than simple sexual pleasure and brief encounters of sexual activity. The average sexual affair endures for two years or less. It often leaves deep emotional scars and memories that are difficult to erase.

Sexual love usually involves a number of factors:

- Sexual desire

- Sexual attraction

- Sexual communication

- Sexual stimulation

- Sexual intercourse

None of these factors requires friendship or spiritual love. All of these factors can be controlled and enhanced, however, by higher forms of love based on commitment, loyalty, trust and mutual respect.

Sexual sin occurs when sexual desire within a person is faced with sexual attraction (whether real, imagined or visually seen) and combined with sexual communication (flirtation, suggestiveness or blatant solicitation) and sexual stimulation (fondling of breasts and genitals) resulting in sexual intercourse outside of marriage.

The desire to experience sexual love is not sinful nor is it wrong to be sexually attracted to a person of the opposite sex. What is wrong is to engage in sexual communication and stimulation with the intent to commit sexual sin. It is definitely wrong to have sexual intercourse with anyone outside of the bonds of marriage.

When People Say, "I Love You"

Not every person can say the words easily. Some refuse

to say it to any person other than the one to whom they get married. Others say it in order to make another person respond well to them. Some choose to use it as a greeting, not believing that it means what others say it does.

Children who are not used to hearing the words, "I love you", from their parents frequently will find it difficult to accept them from others or give them to others. One of the great needs in the families of our society is for the parents to express ... openly and often ... words and actions of love. Parents need to hug and kiss their children each day, and to say those sweet words, "I love you", as often as possible.

When a young person or adult hears the words, "I love you", from a person other than the immediate family, it is interpreted in a variety of ways. It may mean:

- I want to marry you

- I appreciate you.

- I believe in you.

- I treasure your friendship.

- I desire you.

- I am attracted to you.

- I am thankful for you.

- I want to make love to you.

- I want to be your friend.

- I care what happens to you.

It is often difficult for the recipient to know what is meant by the words. In English we might say, "I love ice cream" or, "I love my dog" or, "I love school" or, "I love my work" or, "I love my wife or husband." We mean different things at different times or in different situations.

The potential for hurt and disappointment is great when the recipient of loving words and actions is expecting more than what was intended.

Family Love

Sexual love gives us a feeling of **closeness and intimacy** even if it is just for a moment. Family love gives us a sense of **belonging**. The human personality desires to belong to something or someone that gives us purpose and meaning but even more than that, security.

We join clubs and organizations to experience a measure of family love. It's great to be part of a family that shares common goals, interests and activities. Churches should provide that sense of togetherness, unity and fellowship and that's why we speak of the "family of God".

The Greek word for family love *(storge)* is also used of animals. The offspring share a sense of belonging and togetherness with those animals that brought them into the world. Family love (in Greek thought) existed between parent and child. It involves protection and care. A sense of belonging and a deep, profound security results from the bonds of family love.

On one occasion in the Bible, this word is combined with the word for friendship love in the setting, "*Be kindly affectionate to one another with brotherly love, in honor giving preference to one another*" (Romans 12:10). The words "kindly affectionate" come from the Greek word *philostrogos*, a family relationship that is controlled by friendship love. The words "brotherly love" come from the Greek word *Philadelphia*, furthering the idea of a family by introducing the word for "brother". Christians are admonished to relate to each other as though we were a family – the family of God. Family love provides a sense of belonging and can be adversely affected by selfish attitudes and action.

Family love is hurt and distorted when abuse or neglect occurs. When sexual love occurs between parent and child (incest), family love is damaged and hurt almost beyond recovery. Nothing so destroys a person's sense of belonging and feeling of security as sexual abuse by a parent. It takes years of struggle and pain to restore a person's sense of family when such abuse has occurred.

Neglect can cause tremendous emotional confusion and disorientation. When a parent fails to express love, either with physical affection or verbal appreciation, a child loses the feeling of belonging and feels isolated and alone. It is a terrible feeling to be in a house with parents and children, to be physically a part of a family, but to be emotionally far away. Family love is a tremendous need in all of us. Life is filled with many lonely people, victims of abuse or neglect.

It is well-known that the average person who is involved in chemical dependency (drugs or alcohol) and criminal activity has been a person without strong family love and loyalties. When parents ignore, neglect or abuse their children, they are increasing the potential for serious physical and emotional problems. In some cases these problems extend over a person's entire lifetime, even affecting him in old age.

Many young people become involved in drugs, alcohol and sexual activity because of peer pressure. Without strong family love, they seek this sense of belonging with peer-group friends. Such "groupings" exert enormous pressure upon us to conform. If we refuse, we face the loss of the "family" from which we now derive a sense of security and value. Therefore we need to choose our friends carefully.

Friendship Love

The city of Philadelphia is called the "city of brotherly love" because two Greek words make up its name: "brother" and "love". The word for love is *phile* and is often translated by the word "friend". While sexual love gives us a sense of **intimacy** and family love gives us a sense of **belonging**, it is friendship love that gives us a sense of **value and worth**. When someone desires to be a friend to us, it speaks of our value and worth, at least to that person.

The Bible speaks often of friendship and gives us basic principles to guide us in expressing and enjoying friendship with others. Proverbs 17:17 says, *"A friend loves at all times, and a brother is born for adversity."* True friends are there when you need them and are not affected by bad times or difficult situations. They love at all times.

We are told in Proverbs 18:24, *"A man who has friends must himself be friendly, but there is a friend who sticks closer than a brother."* The opening phrase is difficult to translate. Actually it contains three Hebrew words: many, friends and ruin. Apparently it is a warning about the emotional stress which too many close friendships can bring. The last phrase indicates the importance of a single close friend whose closeness is better than a blood relative.

Friends will cover and protect you when they know things that might be harmful to your reputation (Proverbs 17:9). They realize that gossip is destructive to close friendship. A close friend will confront you when it is needed:

> *Open rebuke is better than love carefully concealed. Faithful are the wounds of a friend, but the kisses of an enemy are deceitful* (Proverbs 27:5,6).

We are exhorted not to forsake our friend but to lean on that person in the time of calamity (Proverbs 27:10) more than we would a relative far away. We are told about the importance of a friend's counsel (Proverbs 27:9), and how gifts will strengthen the friendship (Proverbs 19:4,6).

Jesus used the term *phile* to describe His disciples, emphasizing the importance of loving one another:

Greater love has no one than this, than to lay down one's life for his friends. You are My friends if you do whatever I command you. No longer do I call you servants, for a servant does not know what is master is doing, but I have called you friends, for all things that I heard from My father I have made known to you (John 15:12-15).

We are willing to lay down our lives for the friends we love and to reveal ourselves and our activities to them.

The Greek words *phileo* or *phile* are used frequently in the Bible and are often put with other words to expand the meaning; for example:

- *philagathos* - used once in Titus 1:8 - "a lover of what is good"

- *philadelphia* - used six times - "brotherly love"

- *philadelphos* – used once in I Peter 3:8 – "love as brothers"

- *philandros* – used once in Titus 2:4 – "to love their husbands"

- *philanthropia* – used twice in Acts 18:2 and Titus 3:4 – "love ... toward man"

- *philanthropos* – used once in Acts 27:3 – "treated ... kindly"

- *philarguria* – used once in I Timothy 6:10 – "love of money"

- *philaguros* – used twice in Luke 16:14 and II Timothy 3:2 – "lovers of money"

- *philautos* – used once in II Timothy 3:2 – "lovers of themselves"

- *phileo* – used 25 times – "love" and "kiss"

- *phileedonos* – used once in II Timothy 3:4 – "lovers of pleasure"

- *phileema* – used seven times – "kiss"

- *philia* - used once in James 4:4 - "friendship"

- *philotheos* - used once in II Timothy 3:4 - "lovers of God"

- *philoneikia* - used once in Luke 22:24 - "rivalry"

- *philoneikos* - used once in I Corinthians 11:16 - "contentious"

- *philoxenia* - used twice in Romans 12:13 and Hebrews 13:2 - "given to hospitality"

- *philoxenos* - used three times in I Timothy 3:2, Titus 1:8,1 Peter 4:9 - "hospitable"

- *philoproteuo* - used once in III John 9 - "loves to have the preeminence"

- *philos* - used 29 times - "friend"

- *phiosophia* - used once in Colossians 2:8 - "philosophy" (love of wisdom)

- *philosophos* - used once in Acts 17:18 - "philosophers"

- *philostorgos* – used once in Romans 12:10 – "kindly affectionate"

- *philotekvos* – used once in Titus 2:4 – "love . . . children"

- *philotimeomai* – used three times in Romans 15:20, II Corinthians 5:9, and I Thessalonians 4:11 – "make it our aim" or "aspire"

- philophronos – used once in Acts 28:7 – "courteously"

- *philophron* – used once in I Peter 3:8 – "courteous"

These words show 27 ways to express and describe the love of friendship. Some of them are used in negative ways (such as "lovers of themselves" or "lovers of money" or "lovers of pleasure"). It is interesting to observe that God loves us with the love of friendship. John 16:27 said, "The Father Himself loves *(phileo)* you...." In John 5:20 we read, "The Father loves *(phileo)* the Son. . . ." Friendship love characterizes the love of God the Father for God the Son, and the love of God the Father for us.

Family love provides nurture, care, protection and a sense of belonging. Family love should characterize the relationships of believers in Jesus Christ as Lord and Savior. We are one and we are a family. Within that family love we can develop special friends. Some are social friends with whom we enjoy doing things together that express common interests and activities. We also have friends who share burdens and responsibilities of ministry and work with us. The common tie involves our common goals and efforts to reach them.

People usually have friends from school days or those with whom we interacted in the neighborhoods where we were raised. Circumstances and environments bring us together. Friends can also be created by need and crisis. You were there and another person needed help. The situation drew you together and a friendship developed.

Some of us will go through life with more friends than we can handle, but others will do almost anything to have just one good friend; all of us need friendship. Marital love should provide friendship and companionship; friendship love is critical for a good marriage. You enjoy being together and doing things together. A marriage that is built on sexual love without a good dose of friendship love will suffer and never be quite what it could have been. Many secular marriage counselors insist that couples should learn to be friends before getting involved sexually. Christians, however, believe that not only should couples learn to be friends before being sexually involved, they believe that no sexual intercourse should take place before marriage.

Thousands of people in our society are not married, but still need friends. Married people still need friends outside of their own marital companionship. This is a hard lesson in life and a difficult one to apply since friends can be threats and cause a great deal of hurt and disappointment.

Most of us need a close friend with whom we can share almost anything and still be accepted, loved, appreciated and understood. The need to have such a friend in addition to a marital spouse has long been the subject of research, debate and controversy. Whether that friend is a person of the same sex or the opposite sex, there are dangers to face and problems to handle. Many spouses simply cannot handle the fact that their marital partners need close friends in addition to themselves. They feel rejected and unwanted – insufficient for their partners to be satisfied and contented.

The delicate line between the "loves" of our heart is very thin at times. We can easily move from friendship love to sexual love without even being aware of how it happened. There is a sense in which close friends are attracted to each other, that's why they are close. They like each other and they enjoy communication and activities that bring them together. Yet examples abound where close friends have become sexually involved with each other with no intention of doing so or of hurting anyone in the process.

The words, "I love you", might have been expressed in the arena of family love and friendship love, but may in the context of sexual love take on a whole new set of meanings and values. To "fall in love" with someone is a phrase of romance and usually results in sexual love, even though it began with friendship love.

Close friends who are married to others must be very careful in their relationship and communication. When a person's marriage is being undermined, the friendship is no longer what it should be; it becomes destructive and clearly violates God's principles of marriage and commitment. True friends will always encourage the marriage and family responsibilities of those whom they call friends. They will never do anything to undermine or hurt the marriage or family responsibilities of their friends.

Close friends will be open and transparent with each other concerning their feelings and desires. When sexual love becomes prominent and the relationship centers on the satisfaction or fulfillment of sexual desire, the friendship will experience emotional stress and a diminishing quality of integrity and respect.

Friendship love is a wonderful blessing and can bring rich rewards in terms of biblical self-image. It is also a very difficult matter when the close friend is a person other than your marital spouse. There is a sense in which a married person is not capable or emotionally prepared to experience close friendship with another person unless there is a strong commitment with the marital spouse. It is difficult to know our true motives (cf Jeremiah 17:9,10), and a difficult marriage may be the reason why a close friendship is desired. Without admitting it or realizing it, the close friendship may present to us what the marriage has never been able to accomplish.

Throughout history, from Bible times until the present, people have experienced the dilemma of loving another person in addition to their present spouse. Jacob received Leah as his first wife, but worked many years more to acquire Rachel as his wife as well. The Bible says that "Jacob loved Rachel" (Genesis 29:16-20). The Bible is not condoning having two wives; it simply presents the facts, as difficult as they may be. Deuteronomy 21:15-17 presents the problem of a man having two wives, one loved and the other unloved. It discusses the problem of inheritance rights among the children.

In analyzing David's love for Bathsheba, we clearly recognize that it began with sexual love. In taking another man's wife, the Bible says in II Samuel 11:27, *"But the thing that David had done displeased the Lord.* "After experiencing the death of the baby that resulted from their sexual union, another baby was born named Solomon, and the Bible says, *"And the Lord loved him"* (II Samuel 12:24). God's grace and forgiveness was greater than David and Bathsheba's sin.

David's son, Amnon, had a great love for his sister, Tamar (II Samuel 13:1,2). From the story, it appears that this was sexual love. After forcing her to have sex with him, the Bible then makes it clear that he *"...hated her exceedingly."* His hatred was greater than his former love (II Samuel 13:15). The Bible says of Solomon (I Kings 11:1), *"But King Solomon loved many foreign women."* Verse 2 says, *"Solomon clung to these in love."* These women turned his heart away from the Lord and into idolatry.

It is obvious from the Bible accounts that people "loved" others than the marital spouses they were given. The fact is that we are all capable of having more than one person who becomes the object of our love. The Bible stresses the importance of monogamy and condemns polygamy. Church leaders are to be chosen only if they are "husbands of one wife," or a "one-woman man." Regardless of loving

feelings we may have toward others, we are to be faithful
to our marital spouse until death do us part! No exceptions
allowed without experiencing the judgment of God
Himself!

When a close friend becomes so intimate and desirable
that you are willing to give up on your present marriage in
order to be married to the close friend, you are heading for
great pain and emotional disaster. Friends who honor God's
institution of marriage will never do anything to violate
that sacred trust and vow. You may at one time or another
have a deep love and attraction for someone other than
your spouse, but to forsake your vow or to break your
commitment is a dangerous decision that affects your
integrity and removes the blessing of God from your life.

Sexual love, family love, friendship love – we
experience them all. They are part of human personality
and need. But they all need to be controlled by a higher and
more powerful love which we call spiritual love.

Spiritual Love

The word agape is found throughout Greek literature.
It is a dominant theme in the Bible and applies to all areas
of life and practice. It is the nature of God Himself (I John

4:8) and expresses His character and actions toward us (v. 11), motivating us to do the same toward others.

Agape love is the heart and soul of what God requires of us. All the law and the Prophets hang on two commandments:

> *"You shall love the Lord your God with all your heart, with all your soul, and with all your mind." This is the first and great commandment. And the second is like it: "You shall love your neighbor as yourself* (Matthew 22:27-39).

Jesus said to His disciples that He was giving them a new ("fresh" - new in quality) commandment:

> *A new commandment I give to you, that you love one another; as I have loved you, that you also love one another. By this all will know that you are My disciples, if you have love for one another* (John 13:34,35).

The command to "love one another" appears 16 times in the New Testament. It is spiritual love that is being demanded. We are to give God's love to others at all times and in all situations.

The Bible teaches that spiritual love comes from God and is the result of God's Holy Spirit working in our lives. Spiritual love is not present in or available to non-believers. In order to have spiritual love, we must know God personally and be born again, an act of spiritual awakening that is caused by God.

Beloved, let us love one another, for love is of God; and everyone who loves is born of God and knows God. He who does not love does not know God, for God is love. In this the love of God was manifested toward us, that God has sent His only begotten Son into the world, that we might live through Him. In this is love, not that we loved God, but that He loved us and sent His Son to be the propitiation for our sins. Beloved, if God so loved us, we also ought to love one another (I John 4:7-11).

Some time ago a reputable physician listed several emotions that can produce disease in human beings. At the top of the list was fear, followed by frustration, rage, resentment, hatred, jealousy, envy, self-centeredness and ambition. According to the same physician, the one and only antidote that can save a person from these is ... love!

Augustine said, "What does love look like? It has the hands to help others. It has the feet to hasten to the poor and needy. It has eyes to see misery and want. It has the ears to hear the sighs and sorrows of men. That is what love looks like."

Today it seems that everybody wants love, or at least what they think is love, but so few seem to grasp the uniqueness of the spiritual love that comes only from God. Valentinus, an early theologian after whom Valentine's Day is named, came up with the following statement: "God is all love; but love is not love except there is some object of affection." Unfortunately, Valentinus ignored the physical part of Christ and while he talked a lot about love, he also gave the impression that God was merely love and not much else. This error is repeated even today by those who would look toward God for love without looking to Him in accountability and responsibility.

E.C. McKenzie was right on target when he said that the loneliest place in the world is a human heart where God's love is absent.

There's no doubt that people today are struggling with love. One glance at the newspapers proves that fact. We want romance; we want vibes; we want to feel it. But everybody comes up a little short, a little empty. Some people are perpetually sad or lonely because they have never seen or experienced genuine expressions of love. Many are insecure, others feel rejected. Some are bitter, resentful and empty – all because they have never experienced genuine or spiritual love. We all want love, but do we really know what love is all about?

Two hundred years ago, one well-known encyclopedia discussed the word "atom" with the use of only four lines, while "love" was treated by a five-page discussion. In a more recent edition of the same encyclopedia, five pages were given to the word "atom" while "love" was omitted entirely!

Spiritual Love Is Eternal

According to I Corinthians 13:8, *"Love never fails."* God's love is eternal, not merely temporal. It is not something that man invented, and it is not limited by our experiences in life. God's love is eternal. It supersedes the time in which we live. It had no beginning and it has no end because God Himself is love (I John 4:8). God is not merely love, and love is not God, but God is love.

When the apostle Paul used the words, *"Love never fails",* he employed the use of a double negative in the Greek language. It emphasizes that God's love never, at any time or at any moment, has ever failed. It hasn't failed because it is eternal, not temporal. God's love is eternal because He, Himself, is eternal.

Jeremiah 31:3 quotes the Lord's words about His people when He says, *"I have loved you with an everlasting love."* The Queen of Sheba on her visit to Solomon made this remark: *"The Lord has loved Israel forever"* (I Kings 10:9).

If you want to know this spiritual love, the love that sustains, satisfies, fills your life with joy and endures forever, then you need to know God Himself. God is love but you will never know that personally until you experience a relationship with the eternal God.

Spiritual Love Is Personal

In our world, we tend to love things. We throw the word "love" around loosely because we really do love things. But God's love, this spiritual love, is personal. We read:

Behold what manner of love the Father has bestowed on us, that we should be called children of God! Therefore the world does not know us, because it did not know Him (I John 3:1,2).

*In this the children of God and the children of
the devil are manifest: Whoever does not
practice righteousness is not of God, nor is he
who does not love his brother. For this is the
message that you heard from the beginning, that
we should love one another* (I John 3:10,11).

To those who are the children of God, He has bestowed
on us an incredible, amazing love. It is an intensely personal
love. This passage does not say that he is not a child of God
who does not love his boat, or his bank account, or his
house, or his car, or his job. It says ... *his brother.* This is
personal love!

Deuteronomy 33:3 says, *"Yes, He loves the people."* II
Chronicles 2:11 adds, *"The Lord loves His people."* John
3:16 states, *"For God so loved the world. .. that whoever...."*
God's love is individual persons.

When we love **things**, we are actually giving evidence
that the love of the Father is not in us. Consider this passage:

*Do not love the world or the things in the world.
If anyone loves the world, the love of the Father
is not in him. For all that is in the world – the
lust of the flesh, the lust of the eyes, and the*

pride of life - is not of the Father, but is of the world. And the world is passing away, and the lust of it; but he who does the will of God abides forever (I John 2:15-17).

We tend to love things, to love possessions, even to love people's responses to what we possess. We love the fame and the popularity. Many of us use things to express love. Though love gives, many times what we give is not true evidence of God's love in our hearts since we can be devoid of God's true love in our hearts and still give things.

God, however, loves people and we need to establish this same kind of priority in our lives. Rather than loving the things that people give us, or the things people do for us, or the attention that people give us, we need to love people themselves!

Spiritual Love Is Unusual

Spiritual love does not operate like other kinds of love. For one thing, it does not require a response in order to function. Have you ever noticed that when somebody loves you, you have a natural tendency to love him or her in return? We like to have people love us, and then we respond, but, in a sense, that is an indictment against our selfish concept of love.

In this the love of God was manifested toward us, that God has sent His only begotten Son into the world, that we might live through Him. In this is love, not that we loved God, but that He loved us and sent His Son to be the propitiation for our sins (I John 4:9,10)

We immediately want to love those who already love us, but the real test of love occurs when we meet someone who doesn't like us. In my early months at a church where I pastored, I was shaking hands with people as they left the service. A gentleman whom I had never met said to me, "I don't like you." I was a bit taken back by his abrupt remark and I couldn't think of what to say, so out came the immediate response, "After that, I'm not too fond of you, either!" That was the wrong response (and was corrected!), but it shows the way we usually and naturally respond to people who don't like us.

God's love does not require a response in order to function. God doesn't love you because you love Him. He loves you no matter what. In fact, according to I John 4:19, our very capacity to love exists because He first loved us. Romans 5:8 says,

"God demonstrates His own love toward us, in that while we were still sinners, Christ died for us."

When we didn't care anything about Him, God sent His Son into the world to love us and to die on the cross for our sins, even though we did nothing to earn it or deserve it.

Spiritual love is not only unusual because it doesn't require a response in order to function, but it is also unusual because it is not selfish. When spiritual love controls us, we will often react in a way that is completely opposite to what our culture or natural instincts might dictate. We are admonished constantly in this society, "Watch out for number one," meaning ourselves. Yet God's love will do the opposite.

Two rams, one old and one young, met face-to-face on a narrow mountain ledge. The young ram was ready to go head-to-head with the older ram to see who got passing rights. The older ram knew that if they fought, it was likely that both would end up plunging off the ledge to a horrible death. So, in order to preserve them both, the older ram lay down on the path and let the younger ram walk over him. A simple story, but a powerful point about spiritual love. It allows people to walk all over us!

Spiritual Love Is Practical

Spiritual love is not just flowery language and mushy feelings. It involves real compassion, meeting the needs of others, caring about other people.

Whoever has this world's goods, and sees his brother in need, and shuts up his heart from him, how does the love of God abide in him? My little children, let us not love in word or in tongue, but in deed and in truth (I John 3:17,18).

If we are entirely insensitive to the needs of others, we are giving evidence that the love of God does not control us. We need to understand that the love of God is practical and will respond with compassion to human need. When you have the means to help but you do not do it, spiritual love is absent in you.

Compassion is understanding the troubles of others, coupled with an urgent desire to help. However, we are not naturally compassionate but self-centered; compassion is an attribute we must learn. Compassion is cultivating the ability to put yourself in the shoes of another person, remembering that all the facts and circumstances affecting that person are not known by you. When we don't care what other people's needs are, the love of God does not control us.

Spiritual love is practical; it is described as obedience to the commands of God.

> *By this we know that we love the children of God, when we love God and keep His commandments. For this is the love of God, that we keep His commandments. And His commandments are not burdensome* (I John 5:2,3).

Keeping God's commandments is not legalism – it is freedom! Obedience to God's commands will set you free to be what God wants you to be. The term "His commandments" does not refer to all the many interpretations and applications which religious beliefs might come up with. These commandments are not the Talmudic interpretations or what rabbinical scholars have written; they are what Jesus Christ said. When we follow Him, we will not only understand the law, but we will understand that all of God's Word, with all of its commands, is fulfilled in the one command that we are to love one another (Romans 13:8-10; Galatians 5:13-15). When we follow the commands of Jesus Christ, we will love just as He wants us to.

But what if we don't "feel" it? We don't need to feel it! This generation is into "feelings" as the standard which determines what is right and wrong, but God tells us to do what is right even when we don't feel like it. When we are obedient to God, He will reward us with the feelings that we ought to have because of our obedience.

Selective obedience is not obedience at all; it is merely convenience. When you see a need, you should act out of love whether or not the feelings are there. Do it even though you don't feel like it, and you will have expressed spiritual love, the love of God Himself!

Spiritual Love Is Sacrificial

The heart and depth of spiritual love is contained in the word "sacrifice".

By this we know love, because He laid down His life for us. And we also ought to lay down our lives for the brethren (I John 3:16).

The Greek word for "life" is the same word for "soul". When we have God's love, we are willing to sacrifice our plans, our emotions, our desires, our dreams, etc., for the benefit of those whom we say we love. Dying physically for someone is a deep and powerful expression of love. Jesus said in John 15:13, *"Greater love has no one than this, than to lay down one's life for his friends."* Sometimes we need to learn to sacrifice all those other things and attitudes for the benefit of others. It might mean going shopping when you would have rather gone to a concert! It is doing what others want to do instead of doing what you want to do. Ephesians 5:2 tells us to "... *walk in love, as Christ also has loved and given Himself for us, an offering and a sacrifice to God for a sweet-smelling aroma."* **Love is sacrifice.**

From history, we see an application of this kind of love in the life and times of Cyrus, King of Persia. He was one of the most attractive and handsome monarchs of ancient history with his good looks and eloquence well-documented. When he walked into a room, his presence took it over.

After one of the battles in which Cyrus had achieved a great victory, he gave audience to a young prince he had captured, along with the prince's wife and children. He brought them into his tent, as was customary, to go over the terms of what was going to happen in the light of the battle's outcome. Cyrus looked at the prince, his wife and his children and said, "What will you give me if I set you free?" The prince replied, "I would give you half of everything I own." Cyrus thought for a moment and said, "What would you give me if I set your children free?" The prince replied,

"I would give you all that I possess." Finally Cyrus looked at the prince's beautiful wife and asked, "What will you give me if I set your wife free?" The prince answered, "Sir, if you will only set my wife free, you can kill me." It is recorded that Cyrus was so touched by this show of devotion and sacrifice that he set the prince, his wife and his children free and required nothing from him.

Later that same night as the prince was alone with his wife, he said, "Did you not think that Cyrus was an extremely handsome and articulate man?" His wife looked lovingly at him and replied, "I did not notice. I had eyes only for the one who said he would give his life for me."

Husbands are told, *"Love your wives, just as Christ also loved the church and gave Himself for it"* (Ephesians 5:25). Yet tragically, we see marriages being torn apart by selfishness, families broken apart by self-centeredness and no evidence of spiritual love. God's love is sacrificial and totally different from what we see in our world today.

Some of us remember when the USS Pueblo was captured by the North Koreans and its 82 surviving crew members were thrown into brutal captivity. One incident was the experience of 13 of that crew who one day were required to sit rigidly around a table for hours. Suddenly, after several hours, the door of the room was thrown open and a North Korean guard brutally beat the man in the first chair with the butt of his rifle. The next day, as each man sat in his assigned place, again the door was thrown open and the man in the first chair was brutally beaten. On the third day, the same thing happened to the same man. Knowing that the man probably would not survive another beating, a different young sailor switched places with him. When the door was flung open, the guard automatically beat the new victim senseless. For weeks the process went on and each day a new man stepped forward to sit in that awful chair, knowing full well what would happen. At last the guards gave up in exasperation. They could not defeat that kind of sacrificial love.

Spiritual Love Is Unconditional

The word "if" is applied to the words of love so often that we have become accustomed to believing that love is always conditional, that it will be there if conditions are met. Love often comes with expectations; that's why divorce becomes such an easy alternative for so many people – it is a natural avenue for conditional love gone sour. Spiritual love, however, is unconditional, and is based on three things:

- Spiritual love is based on God's faithfulness.

God speaks His Word and does not cancel it. Deuteronomy 7:6-9 contains this marvelous truth:

> *For you are a holy people to the Lord your God;*
> *the Lord your God has chosen you to be a people*
> *for Himself, a special treasure above all the*
> *peoples on the face of the earth. The Lord did not*
> *set His love on you nor choose you because you*
> *were more in number than any other people, for*
> *you were the least of all peoples; but because the*
> *Lord loves you, and because He would keep the*
> *oath which He swore to your fathers, the Lord*
> *has brought you out with a mighty hand, and*
> *redeemed you from the house of bondage, from*
> *the hand of Pharaoh, king of Egypt. Therefore,*
> *know that the Lord your God, He is God, the*
> *faithful God who keeps covenant and mercy for*
> *a thousand generations with those who love*
> *Him and keep His commandments.*

God's love is unconditional; it is not based on human performance or worth, but rather on His own attribute of faithfulness. God made a promise and He will keep it:

> *Through the Lord's mercies we are not*
> *consumed, because His compassions fail not.*

They are new every morning; great is Your faithfulness (Lamentations 3:22,23).

In the Bible, marriage is to be based on spiritual love, the love that is unconditional. It is rooted in faithfulness. You spoke a vow and you are to keep your vow just as God keeps every word that He has spoken. Spiritual love does not set up a list of demands, expectations or conditions. There is no "if clause" in its applications.

• Spiritual love is based on God's mercy.

Mercy holds back from us what we really deserve. God knows what we are like, yet He still loves us unconditionally. Some people think that the sin and junk in their lives is keeping God from loving them, but that is simply not true. God loves you, and where sin abounds, His grace abounds much more (Romans 5:20). His mercy holds back from us what we really deserve and His grace gives us what we do not deserve. God loves us in spite of what we are or what we have done against Him.

In Psalm 103:8-14 there is a beautiful description of spiritual love, connecting it with the mercy of God:

The Lord is merciful and gracious, slow to anger, and abounding in mercy. He will not always

strive with us, nor will He keep His anger
forever. He has not dealt with us according to
our sins, nor punished us according to our
iniquities. For as the heavens are high above the
earth, so great is His mercy toward those who
fear Him; as far as the east is from the west, so
far has He removed our transgressions from us.
As a father pities his children, so the Lord pities
those who fear Him. For He knows our frame;
He remembers that we are dust.

The unconditional love of God, what we call "spiritual
love", is based upon the mercy of God. We are told by Jesus
Christ in Luke 6:36, *"Therefore be merciful, just as your*
Father also is merciful."

Many of us operate differently. When we are wronged,
we want to retaliate rather than to show mercy. We
sometimes believe that we are God's instrument for
showing people how wrong they are! Some people believe
they are like the weapons of God, commissioned to
administer justice and vengeance upon those who have
wronged us. We don't like to be treated poorly and we
usually think that we deserve more than we actually do.

If spiritual love controls us, we will be able to love people
unconditionally by basing our words and actions upon the

mercy of God. Even if another person has wronged us repeatedly, even if he or she is unlovable, even if he has done nothing to deserve mercy and love, we are to love him without any thought of revenge or getting even. That is showing mercy. That is reflecting the love of God! If we all received what we deserved, we would be doomed for eternity in hell!

- Spiritual love is based on God's forgiveness.

Proverbs 10:12 says, *"Love covers all sins."* Proverbs 17:9 tells us *"He who covers a transgression seeks love, but he who repeats a matter separates the best of friends."* In Ephesians 4:32 we are told, *"Be kind to one another, tenderhearted, forgiving one another, even as God in Christ forgave you."* I Peter 4:8 says, *"Above all things have fervent love for one another, for love will cover a multitude of sins."*

A friend of Clara Barton (founder of the American Red Cross) once reminded her of a cruel thing that had been done to her years before. Miss Barton, however, did not seem to recall it. "Don't you remember?" her friend insisted. "No," Miss Barton replied, "I distinctly remember forgetting it!"

Spiritual love is characterized by forgiveness. Jesus told His disciples the following about forgiveness:

*If your brother sins against you, rebuke him;
and if he repents, forgive him. And if he sins
against you seven times a day, and seven times
in a day returns to you, saying, "I repent, "you
shall forgive him* (Luke 17:3,4).

Repeated offenses are hard to forgive (and forget!) but
when spiritual love is controlling us, forgiveness will be
applied no matter how often the offense has occurred.

The standard for forgiveness (Colossians 3:13) is, *"Even
as Christ forgave you, so you also must do."* Jesus Christ has
forgiven all the sins of those who believe in Him. No matter
how terrible their lifestyle and their rebellion against God,
when they trust in His work of salvation, they are forgiven.
On the basis of our Lord's unconditional forgiveness toward
us, we are to forgive others as well.

Grace gives us what we do not deserve; mercy holds
back from us what we do deserve; forgiveness is refusing to
demand revenge, payment or humiliation. It restores and
responds like nothing ever happened. It covers, protects
and forgets.

Spiritual Love Is Supernatural

After reading about spiritual love, we can become totally frustrated. Can any person actually experience this? Is it possible for fallible, vulnerable, inconsistent human beings to experience and enjoy spiritual love? It seems beyond the reach of us all; it is a standard too difficult to attain, a practice too impossible to apply at all times and in all situations. It seems to be totally different from natural impulse and normal human behavior.

Ephesians 3:19 says that this love *"...passes (or surpasses) knowledge"*. The Bible teaches that a spiritual awakening and a personal knowledge of God Himself are requirements for experiencing true spiritual love:

> *Beloved, let us love one another, for love is of God; and everyone who loves is born of God and knows God. He who does not love does not know God, for God is love* (I John 4:7,8).

We must know God personally in order to experience spiritual love. Romans 5:5 says that this love is *"...poured out in our hearts by the Holy Spirit who was given to us."* Galatians 5:22 calls it a *"fruit of the Spirit".* I John 5:1 states, *"Whoever believes that Jesus is the Christ is born of God, and everyone who loves Him who begot also loves him who is begotten of Him."*

Left to ourselves, it is impossible for us to love people in this way. According to the Bible, no matter how smart we are, no matter how much we have experienced in life and no matter how much we think we know about love, God's love surpasses the human ability to understand it and to apply it. Its dimensions are so vast that it is impossible for any one person to comprehend it or demonstrate it without God's help. According to Scripture, we need to be "born of God"; that is, we need a spiritual awakening that comes only through a personal relationship with God's Son, Jesus Christ our Lord. This personal relationship with God comes only through faith in Him who loved us so much that He died on the cross for our sins, and rose again from the dead, thus guaranteeing that we will live forever with Him!

For every believer who has already begun a relationship with Jesus Christ, there is something very important to understand about spiritual love: Our capacity to experience it is brought to us by this personal relationship with Jesus Christ, but our ability to express it continually in our lives toward others depends upon the work of the Holy Spirit who lives within us. One of the great weaknesses of the

Christian life is trying to move and operate under our own
power, trying to live the Christian life in our own strength.
The love we desperately need and for which we long in our
own hearts is produced by the Holy Spirit and given to those
who walk in obedience to God's Word.

The Genuine Article

Where do we go for love today? According to television
and movies, we should look for love in the fleeting, hollow,
meaningless relationships acted out on the screen. But we
know from the broken lives and shattered dreams of the
actors and actresses themselves that no answers can be
found there.

According to the love gurus and proponents of the so-
called "new morality", we should look for love in fleeting
sexual gratification, in the selfish satisfaction of animal
passion and self-indulgence. However, in a world plagued
by sexual disease, illegitimate pregnancies and the atrocity
of abortion, it is obvious that genuine love is not the product
of that philosophy.

Regardless of the various answers and dead-end
avenues which the world proposes, the Bible clearly teaches
that real love, the genuine article that fulfills the deepest
longings and needs of the human heart, can be found only

in God Himself, through a personal relationship with His
Son, Jesus Christ our Lord.

Have you come to know Him? Have you ever made a
personal commitment of your life and future to the One
Who died on the cross for your sins, the One Who made you
and knows all about you and still loves you? There is no
greater love available to you than this love with which He
will fill your life.

Sexual love, family love and friendship love are made
beautiful, fulfilling and deeply rewarding when they are
controlled by spiritual love – the love of God Himself.

> Love Divine, all loves excelling,
>> Joy of heaven to earth come down;
> Fix in us Thy humble dwelling,
>> All Thy faithful mercies crown.
> Jesus, Thou art all compassion;
>>> Pure, unbounded love Thou art.
> Visit us with Thy salvation;
>>> Enter every trembling heart.

PART TWO

The Problem of Love

Chapter Two

The Problem of Love

Should We Love Ourselves?

Our culture is dominated by the belief that a person cannot love others until he loves himself. It permeates our bookstores, in both secular and Christian literature. We are given detailed instruction on how to love ourselves and increase our worth and potential.

Christian writers insist that the Bible encourages us to love ourselves. The favorite quoted passage is:

You shall love the Lord your God with all your heart, with all your soul, and with all your mind. This is the first and great commandment. And the second is like it: You shall love your neighbor as yourself. On these two commandments hang all the Law and the Prophets (Matthew 22:37-40).

Christian psychologists refer to the words of our Lord
Jesus Christ and insist that He instructed us to love
ourselves. Self-love is promoted as the key to an effective
and meaningful life. We are told that the major reason we
do not have loving relationships with others is because we
have low self-esteem. We simply do not love ourselves, but
Jesus did not instruct us to love ourselves; instead, He
assumes that we already do. The grammatical construction
is urging us to love others like we already do love ourselves.

Ephesians 5:29 says, *"No one ever hated his own flesh,
but nourishes and cherishes it, just as the Lord does the
church."* No one hates himself. That's what the Bible says.

The New Commandment

What Jesus commanded us to do was to "love one
another":

*A new commandment I give to you, that you love
one another; as I have loved you, that you also
love one another. By this all will know that you
are My disciples, if you have love for one
another* (John 13:34,35).

Sixteen times we are told to "love one another". Jesus repeated His "new commandment":

This is My commandment, that you love one another as I have loved you (John 15:12).

These things I command you, that you love one another (John 15:17).

The apostle Paul wrote:

Concerning brotherly love you have no need that I should write to you, for you yourselves are taught by God to love one another (I Thessalonians 4:9).

It was well-known among the early Christians that the major biblical priority is to love one another.

John wrote:

This is the message that you heard form the beginning, that we should love one another (I John 3:1).

This is His commandment: that we should believe on the name of His Son Jesus Christ and love one another, as He gave us commandment (I John 3:23).

This commandment we have from Him: that He who loves God must love his brother also (I John 4:2).

Whoever believes that Jesus is the Christ is born of God, and everyone who loves Him who begot also loves him who is begotten of Him. By this we know that we love the children of God, when we love God and keep His commandments. For this is the love of God, that we keep His commandments. And His commandments are not burdensome (I John 5:1-3).

Romans 13:8-10 tells us that all of God's law is fulfilled by keeping this new commandment of Jesus Christ:

Owe no one anything except to love one another, for he who loves another has fulfilled the Law. For the commandments are, "You shall not commit adultery," "You shall not murder," "You shall not steal," "You shall not bear false witness," "You shall not covet," and if there is any other commandment, all are summed up in this saying, namely, "You shall love your neighbor as yourself."

*You, brethren, have been called to liberty; only
do not use liberty as an opportunity for the flesh,
but through love serve one another. For all the
law is fulfilled in one word, even in this : "You
shall love your neighbor as yourself* (Galatians
5:13-5).

The evidence is overwhelming: The Bible does not urge
self-love; it assumes it. Instead, the Bible commands us to
love others. The "new commandment" does not mean new
from the standpoint of time because it was taught in the Old
Testament as well. Leviticus 19:18 says, *"You shall love your
neighbor as yourself*:*I am the Lord."* In Greek there are two
words for "new." One refers to new in time, and the other
refers to new in quality. We would use the word "fresh".
That word appears in the passages referring to the "new
commandment" of our Lord Jesus Christ. It was given in a
new and fresh way. What made it new in quality was the
standard by which it should be applied. Jesus said, "...*as I
have loved you"*. His example of love is now the basis upon
which all efforts to love others can be evaluated.

Consider the following facts about the new commandment to love one another.

- It is the main TRUTH of the Old Testament law. See Deuteronomy 6:5; Leviticus 19:18; Matthew 22:37-40.

- It is the clear TEACHING of Jesus Christ. See Matthew 5:43-48; John 13:34,35; 15:12,17.

- It is the constant TESTIMONY of the writers of the New Testament.

> Paul - Galatians 5:13,14.
> James - James 2:8
> Peter -1 Peter 1:22; 4:8.
> John -I John 3:11; 4:7-11.

- It is the real TEST of a believer. See I John 2:9-11; 3:10-15,4:7-11,20,21; 5:1-3.

- It is the main TASK of believers toward one another. See John 13:34,35; I Thessalonians 4:9.

The responsibility to love others is a serious matter. Since it is a command of our Lord Jesus Christ, it involves the matter of our obedience to Him whom we call Lord and Savior. I Peter 1:22 emphasizes the intensity of that love for one another:

Since you have purified your souls in obeying the truth through the Spirit in sincere love of the brethren, love one another fervently with a pure heart.

Above all things have fervent love for one another, for love will cover a multitude of sins (I Peter 4:8).

The word, "fervently", comes from a root word meaning "to stretch" and a preposition meaning "out". "To stretch out" indicates an intense or strenuous effort. To love one another the way God wants us to do takes hard work!

The "one another" (Greek - *allelon*) relationships are mentioned 100 times in the Bible. Our responsibilities are spelled out in great detail in terms of both attitudes and actions. The very words, "one another", condemn the proponents of self-love.

The message of the Bible concerning the self is the exact opposite of current cultural opinions. Jesus said:

If anyone desires to come after Me, let him deny himself, and take up his cross daily, and follow Me (Luke 9:23).

To "take up the cross" involves a one-way trip to death. The Bible's message about self is "deny yourself". That is a far cry from the message of self-love which is propagated so extensively in our society.

Self-preservation is not the message of the Bible. We are urged to lay down our lives for those we love (I John 3:16). Jesus said,

> *"Whoever desires to save his life will lose it, but whoever loses his life for My sake will save it"* (Luke 9: 24).

Jesus taught us,

> *"Greater love has no one than this, than to lay down one's life for his friends"* (John 15:13).

Acceptance in Spite of Differences

We usually find it easy to love those who agree with us. Those who emphasize the importance of loving yourself first will insist that we do not need to endure the differences, disappointments or disagreements of others. We are told, "You have to think of yourself first!" This leads many people to divorce court. Their idea of love is to find someone who agrees with them and will give them "space", and someone who will not do anything to thwart their personal goals and ambitions in life.

In Romans 14:1 to 15:13 there is a lengthy discussion about the differences among Christians and how we need to learn to love each other in spite of those disagreements. The arguments center around diet, the disagreements between vegetarian and non-vegetarians, and the celebration of special days. All of these are non-essentials that divide Christians from one another.

The basic admonition is:

Receive one who is weak in the faith, but not to dispute over doubtful things (Romans 14:1).

Therefore receive one another, just as Christ also received us, to the glory of God (Romans 15:7).

The New American Standard Bible translates the word "receive" as "accept".

Learning to accept one another when there are minor disagreements is a quality of God's love. If we can't agree to disagree on non-essentials, we will not get far in our attempts to love others. Some things are worth fighting and dying for, but other things you can take or leave. Good Bible teachers sometimes disagree on the interpretation of various passages in the Bible. It is foolish for any one of us to think that we have the ultimate truth on any given passage! We do our best, but there are times when we must be gracious and kind toward those who disagree with us.

We being many, are one body in Christ, and individually members of one another (Romans 12:5).

The teaching of the body with its many members appears frequently in Paul's writing, and a rather lengthy discussion is found in I Corinthians 12. Each member is a part of the overall body and has a spiritual gift to use in building up other members of the body. We must learn to accept the ministries of others even though they may be quite different from our own. We do not all have the same gifts; there is diversity in the body.

I Corinthians 12:4-6 points out the differences in the use of spiritual gifts:

There are diversities of gifts, but the same spirit. There are differences of ministries, but the same

*Lord. And there are diversities of activities, but it
is the same God who works all in all.*

The diversities or differences involve the number and
nature of the gifts, how they are used and the results that
God works through them. If two people have the gift of
teaching, it does not mean that they will use it in exactly the
same way. One may prefer to teach adults while the other
may prefer to teach children. One may be more effective
teaching a thousand people while the other might be more
effective teaching ten people.

I Corinthians 12:14-27 lays out the importance of our
differences and the necessity of accepting every member of
the body and seeing the importance of every bodily
function. Consider the following insights from this passage:

- The body is not one member but many.

- No one member can conclude that it is not a part of
  the body.

- God has put the members in the body as He pleased.

- Although there are many members, there is only one
  body.

- No member can say that another member is
  not needed.

- The insignificant parts of the body should
  receive greater honor.

- There is to be no division in the body.

- Members are to care for one another.

- The body belongs to Jesus Christ.

I John 1:7 tells us that all believers *have "...fellowship with one another"*. That eliminates excluding any believer. All are to be loved and accepted in spite of minor differences and disagreements.

The word "fellowship" refers to that which we share in common. Although used in a variety of ways in the New Testament, the context of I John 1 reveals that the "fellowship" we have with each other is the fact that we all share the life of God within each believer. Many of us do not enjoy the fellowship we have, but it is nevertheless a positional fact: We already do have fellowship with all true believers. If a person has come to know Jesus Christ as his Lord and Savior, then we are one with him in the body of

Christ; we have fellowship with him, and should accept
him without hesitation or reservation.

Reasons for Non-acceptance

Some of the problems I have observed in Christians
accepting one another may seem to some people to be
ridiculous, but to others, they are real problems. Take a
moment and reflect on these problems as possible
hindrances to our acceptance of others, barriers to loving
them as God wants us to love them.

- **Racial differences.** The color of a person's skin
  should never cause us to refuse fellowship. To
  describe humanity as "races" based on skin
  color is ridiculous and certainly not biblical.
  All peoples of the world have descended from
  the three sons of Noah. The Canaanites were
  condemned by God for their immorality and
  idolatry, not for their skin color. The
  Canaanites were not "black people", but were
  more "brown" and Semitic in culture and
  appearance. Canaan was involved in immoral
  conduct in the case of his grandfather, and
  thus received a curse from God upon his
  descendants (cf. Genesis 9:20-27). The curse

that was placed upon Noah's grandson, Canaan, has already been fulfilled in history. The Canaanites have been destroyed and the prophecy fulfilled.

The hostility and barriers between whites and blacks that characterize our secular society should never be seen among the people of God. Paul said:

He has made from one blood every nation of men to dwell on all the face of the earth, and has determined their preappointed times and the boundaries of their habitation (Acts 17:26).

We have a common ancestor and God's plan was to divide people into nations, languages, tribes and families. God has determined in advance how long these nations will exist and how much territory they will possess.

The proper Christian principle is:

There is neither Jew nor Greek, there is neither slave nor free, there is neither male nor female; for you are all one in Christ Jesus (Galatians 3:2).

- **Economic differences**. Some churches are described as being "upper-middle-class" or "lower-class". Such distinctions are anti-biblical and violate the new commandment to love one another. Churches are often characterized by their homogeneous unit, that distinctiveness that represents most of the people. We are sometimes even urged to do evangelism and ministry among those people who are most like us and avoid others who are culturally distinct.

James condemns the practice of showing partiality based on economics:

My brethren, do not hold the faith of our Lord Jesus Christ, the Lord of Glory, with partiality. For if there should come into your assembly a man with gold rings, in fine apparel, and there should also come in a poor man in filthy clothes, and you pay attention to the one wearing the fine clothes and say to him, "You sit here in a good place," and say to the poor man, "You stand there," or "Sit here at my footstool," have you not shown partiality among yourselves, and become judges with evil thoughts? Listen, my beloved brethren : Has God not chosen the poor of this world to be rich in faith and heirs of the kingdom which He promised to those who love Him? But you have dishonored the poor man. Do not the rich oppress you and drag you into the courts? Do they not blaspheme that noble name by which you are called? If you really fulfill the royal law according to the Scripture, "You shall love your neighbor as yourself," you do well; but if you show partiality, you commit sin, and are convicted by the law as transgressors. For whoever shall keep the whole law, and yet stumble in one point, he is guilty of all. For He who said, "Do not commit adultery," also said, "Do not murder." Now if you do not commit adultery, but you do murder, you have become a transgressor of the law. So speak and so do as those who will be judged by the law of liberty. For judgment is without mercy to the one who has shown no mercy. Mercy triumphs over judgment (James 2:1-13).

To love others, we must fully accept them into our fellowship and relationships. To do otherwise is showing partiality and is the opposite of the new commandment.

- **Doctrinal differences.** We are not referring to the doctrines that are essential for our salvation. The problem in Romans 14 dealt with diet and days. Romans 14:19 states:

Let us pursue the things which make for peace and the things by which one may edify another.

Romans 15:1,2 adds:

We then who are strong ought to bear with the scruples of the weak, and not to please ourselves. Let each of us please his neighbor for his good, leading to edification.

That is the opposite of self-love! Self-love seeks ways in which to please self. The Bible tells us to focus on pleasing others rather than ourselves, and to seek to edify or build up other believers. We are told in Romans 15:3, *"Even Christ did not please Himself."*

Those who are vegetarians should not be judged by those who are meat-eaters and vice versa. God's love should rule and overrule in all matters of doctrinal differences regarding nonessentials.

Christians fight over many doctrinal issues, including the use of spiritual gifts, the interpretation of Bible prophecies and even methods of evangelism and discipleship. Where is the love of God in all of these disagreements?

To agree to disagree and still love each other is the highest mark of Christian maturity.

•   **Cultural differences**. Some of the most difficult relationships among believers deal with cultural preferences and differences. This is quite evident in terms of musical styles and tastes. An older generation prefers the music they were used to hearing when they were growing up, while the younger generation prefers musical styles that are more contemporary and great misunderstandings and accusations occur because of these cultural differences.

Dress styles become points of controversy and division in many countries and cultures. Methods of ministry can be points of division and the way a worship service is conducted. In all of these problems, do we understand the new commandment? We are to love one another in spite of our differences.

Godly Actions and Attitudes

Loving yourself is the problem, not the priority! Loving yourself keeps you from seeing your responsibilities toward others and from obedience to our Lord's new commandment. We need several qualities of the love of God in our relationships with other believers.

- **An attitude of humility**. When we are filled with the Holy Spirit, we will be characterized by humility or "submitting to one another" (Ephesians 5:21).

Likewise you younger people, submit yourselves to your elders. Yes, all of you be submissive to one another, and be clothed with humility, for "God resists the proud, but gives grace to the humble." Therefore humble yourselves under the mighty hand of God, that He may exalt you in due time (I Peter 5:5,6).

Humble yourselves in the sight of the Lord, and He will lift you up (James 4:10).

There are three things that are involved in an attitude of humility:

- The importance of others

- The needs of others

- The respect for others

In Philippians 2:3,4 we have a definition of humility:

Let nothing be done through selfish ambition or conceit, but in lowliness of mind let each esteem others better than himself. Let each of you look out not only for his own interests, but also for the interests of others.

When we treat others in this way, we are reflecting the love of God Himself. When you regard others as more important than yourself, and their interests as your interests, you are manifesting humility.

Humility and submission means accepting the advice and counsel of others when it is different from your own opinions and viewpoints. Humility is allowing others to speak before yourself. Humility is playing a game with your children that they like but you don't. Humility is praising others rather than yourself. Humility is listening when you already know what the other person is saying. Humility is complimenting others in a given project that you were responsible for, and for which you put forth great effort.

Humility is beautifully portrayed for us when Jesus washed the feet of His disciples at the Last Supper:

> *If I then, your Lord and Teacher, have washed your feet, you also ought to wash one another's feet. For I have given you an example, that you would do as I have done to you. Most assuredly, I say to you, a servant is not greater than his master; nor is he who is sent greater than he who sent him. If you know these things, happy are you **if you do them** (John 13:14–17).*

Blessing (happiness) comes to those who "**do** these things", not simply those who "**know** these things". Many of us know that we ought to serve others, and that it requires humility to do so, but only in the actual doing of it is there the blessedness and the demonstration of love. Washing feet is a dirty and menial task, but if our Lord was willing to do it, should we not be willing also? Is there any task or service for another believer that you simply will not humble yourself to do?

A Christian friend called upon one of the members of his church who had been confined to his home because of illness. He had a nurse who was paid to come in and help him but who, for one reason or another, had quit. The sick person was bedridden and needed help in every area, including urine and bowel movements. The day after the nurse quit, this friend showed up to bring some encouragement to his sick friend.

Needless to say, the man was in bad shape. The room smelled terrible, and there was quite a mess. My Christian friend took the time to clean everything up and to care for the needs of this sick person and even arranged for further nursing care. That's what I call true love: A willingness to serve and to humble yourself in caring for others. It was not an easy chore, but it was Christian love that responded. Jesus said:

You know that those who are considered rulers over the Gentiles lord it over them, and their great ones exercise authority over them. Yet it shall not be so among you; but whoever desires to become great among you shall be your servant. And whoever of you desires to be first

shall be slave of all. For even the Son of Man did
not come to be served, but to serve and to give
His life a ransom for many (Mark 10:42-45).

Humility is the desire to be a "slave of all". The example
of our Lord is powerful. Philippians 2:8 says,

"He humbled Himself and became obedient to
the point of death, even the death of the cross."

- **A commitment to integrity.** Integrity includes
  many qualities that are needed in our
  relationships with others. The new
  commandment demands that we do
  everything with integrity. Issues of integrity
  include honesty, loyalty, trust and honor.

To love others requires honesty in what we say and do.
It is the natural tendency of the human heart to cover up,
justify, defend and hide. Deceit rests within us all. Jeremiah
17:9 says,

"The heart is deceitful above all things, and
desperately wicked; who can know it?"

We do not know ourselves, nor is the pursuit of such
knowledge a worthwhile goal, but God knows us and

reveals in His Word what we are like. He says that we need His love controlling us.

> *Do not lie to one another, since you have put off*
> *the old man with his deeds* (Colossians 3:9).

> *Therefore, putting away lying, each one speak*
> *truth with his neighbor, for we are members of*
> *one another* (Ephesians 4:25).

Ephesians 4:15 tells us to speak the truth in love. James 4:11,12 warns of how we often treat others, and insists that we have no right to do so:

> *Do not speak evil of one another, brethren. He*
> *who speaks evil of a brother and judges his*
> *brother speaks evil of the law and judges the*
> *law. But if you judge the law, you are not a doer*
> *of the law but a judge. There is one Lawgiver,*
> *who is able to save and to destroy. Who are you*
> *to judge another?*

Critical remarks, cutting statements, and tearing people down are detrimental to our relationships and violations of the new commandment. Integrity refuses to attack and speak evil of others.

Integrity means that you honor other people, rather than yourself. Romans 13:7 says to give honor to whom honor is due. Husbands are told to give *"...honor to the wife, as to the weaker vessel, and as being heirs together of the grace of life, that your prayers may not be hindered"*(I Peter 3:7). Concerning those members of the body which seem less important than others, I Corinthians 12:23 states, *"Those members of the body which we think to be less honorable, on these we bestow greater honor."*

Integrity means that people can trust you. It means that a person's reputation is in safe hands and will be defended by you when that person is not around. Proverbs 17:9 says,

"He who covers a transgression seeks love, but he who repeats a matter separates the best of friends."

Love protects, defends, covers, and seeks to remain loyal.

• A willingness to forgive.

Be kind to one another, tenderhearted, forgiving one another, just as God in Christ also forgave you (Ephesians 4:32).

The word "forgiving" is the Greek word for "grace". Grace gives to us what we do not deserve. True forgiveness is "gracing" others. We are often hesitant to forgive another person because we do not believe that he or she deserves it. Perhaps his words or actions have really hurt us, and we find that the bitterness and resentment in our hearts will not allow us to forgive him.

The way to deal with forgiveness is to remember the example of Jesus Christ: We are to forgive as He has forgiven us.

"Bearing with one another, and forgiving one another, if anyone has a complaint against another; even as Christ forgave you, so you also must do" (Colossians 3:13).

We have natural propensity to seek revenge when we are hurt, or when another person's actions have disappointed us or attacked us personally in some way.

Do not say, "I will recompense evil"; wait for the Lord, and He will save you (Proverbs 20:22).

Repay no one evil for evil. Have regard for good things in the sight of all men. If it is possible, as much as depends on you, live peaceably with all men. Beloved, do not avenge yourselves, but rather give place to wrath; for it is written, "Vengeance is Mine, I will repay," says the Lord (Romans 12:17-19).

As long as we seek to get revenge or to make the person who offended us pay for it, we will not be able to forgive the way the Lord wants us to.

The discretion of a man makes him slow to anger, and it is to his glory to overlook a transgression (Proverbs 19:11).

He who covers a transgression seeks love, but he who repeats a matter separates the best of friends (Proverbs 17:9).

The need in applying forgiveness is to overlook and cover what another has done. When we repeat the matter or continue to expose it, it reveals that we have not forgiven the person at all.

Jesus taught us concerning forgiveness:

Take heed to yourselves. If your brother sins against you, rebuke him; and if he repents, forgive him. And if he sins against you seven

*times a day, and seven times in a day returns to you, saying,
"I repent," you shall forgive him* (Luke 17:3,4).

Most of us refuse to forgive when there have been
repeated offenses. Jesus told us to forgive our brother
"seventy times seven" (Matthew 18:22). He taught us:

> *So My heavenly Father also will do to you if each
> of you, from his heart, does not forgive his
> brother his trespasses* (Matthew 18:25).

- **A dedication to ministry**. Galatians 5:13 says,
  "Through love serve one another." I Peter
  4:9-11 lays out the principles of ministry to
  one another:

> *Be hospitable to one another without grumbling,
> as each one has received a gift, minister it to one
> another, as good stewards of the manifold grace
> of God. If anyone speaks, let him speak as the
> oracles of God. If anyone ministers, let him do it
> as with the ability which God supplies, that in
> all things God may be glorified through Jesus
> Christ, to Whom belong the glory and dominion
> forever and ever.*

The ministry of the believer is fundamental to the growth of the body of Christ. Ephesians 4:12 tells us that the gifted believers given to the church are for the *"...equipping of the saints for the work of ministry, for the edifying of the body of Christ."* This edification is done in the sphere of Christian love (Ephesians 4:16).

We are exhorted to *"edify one another"* (I Thessalonians 5:11), and are told that *"love edifies"* (I Corinthians 8:1).

Let no corrupt communication proceed out of your mouth, but what is good for necessary edification, that it may impart grace to the hearers (Ephesians 4:29).

Let each of us please his neighbor for his good, leading to edification (Romans 15:2).

A dedication to ministry means that we seek to build up other believers, not tear them down. That includes prayer. James 5:16 tells us to *"...pray for one another."*

Ephesians 6:18 says, *"Praying always with all prayer and supplication in the Spirit, being watchful to this end with all perseverance and supplication for all the saints."*

Colossians 4:2 says, *"Continue earnestly in prayer, being vigilant in it with thanksgiving."*

I Thessalonians 5:17 says to *"...pray without ceasing."*

A wonderful example of the kind of prayer that builds up the believer and manifests the love of God in ministry is that found in Colossians 1:9-12:

For this reason we also, since the day we heard it, do not cease to pray for you, and to ask that you may be filled with the knowledge of His will in all wisdom and spiritual understanding that you may have a walk worthy of the Lord, fully pleasing Him, being fruitful in every good work and increasing in the knowledge of God; strengthened with all might, according to His glorious power, for all patience and longsuffering with joy; giving thanks to the Father, Who has qualified us to be partakers of the inheritance of the saints in the light.

• **A desire to encourage.** Nothing so affects our obedience to the new commandment and reveals our concern for others as the desire to encourage or give counsel and comfort. Paul wrote:

I long to see you, that I may impart to you some
spiritual gift, so that you may be established, that
I may be encouraged together with you by the
mutual faith both of you and me (Romans
1:11,12).

I Thessalonians 2:11 speaks of Paul's ministry,

You know how we exhorted, and comforted,
and charged every one of you, as a father does
his own children.

I Thessalonians 4:18 tells us to *"...comfort one another"*
concerning the death of loved ones by reminding them of
the resurrection of the dead and the return of Jesus Christ
for His own. I Thessalonians 5:11 says, *"Comfort each*
other."

The word translated "comfort" or "encouragement" or
"counsel" comes from a Greek word *(parakaleo)* which
means "one called alongside" to help. The Holy Spirit is
called the Comforter or Paraclete. II Corinthians 1:3-7
speaks of such a desire to comfort:

Blessed be the God and Father of our Lord Jesus
Christ, the Father of mercies and God of all
comfort, Who comforts us in all our tribulation,

that we may be able to comfort those who are in any trouble, with the comfort with which we ourselves are comforted by God. For as the sufferings of Christ abound in us, so our consolation also abounds through Christ. Now if we are afflicted, it is for your consolation and salvation, which is effective for enduring the same sufferings which we also suffer. Or if we are comforted, it is for your consolation and salvation. And our hope for you is steadfast, because we know that as you are partakers of the sufferings, so also you will partake of the consolation.

God is the *"God of all comfort"* and is *the "Father of mercies."* Giving encouragement to other believers is a practical demonstration of the new commandment. We truly love one another when we encourage each other.

I went to a hospital room one day to give encouragement to a dying believer. Little did I realize when I walked into the room that the one who would do the most encouraging was that dying believer, not me! That person's hope and confidence in the Lord made a deep impression on my soul. I cannot forget it; it encourages my heart whenever I think about the incident. I pray that I will be the same kind of blessing to others when I am at death's door!

Don't you love to be around people who are always encouraging others? I have a friend in the ministry who is like that; he is such a joy to be around because he is always encouraging others. It's contagious: You want to minister to others because of what he's done for you.

One of the most difficult sides to the ministry of encouragement and counsel is when you must confront a brother or sister in the Lord who has fallen into a sinful lifestyle. The Bible uses the word "admonish" or "warn" to describe this difficult responsibility. The Greek word *nouthesia* or *noutheteo* is used 11 times in the New Testament. I Corinthians 10:11 reminds us that the things written in the Old Testament were written for our admonition. In Ephesians 6:4 the word appears in the responsibility of fathers raising their children. They are responsible for discipline and admonition.

The apostle Paul said in Acts 20:31 that he continually warned the believers with many tears. Admonishment needs a sensitive and broken heart. Romans 15:14 says that those who admonish need to be filled with goodness and knowledge. Paul spoke about the importance of a father's heart in I Corinthians 4:14 when we try to warn others. In Colossians 1:28 and 3:16 we are told to warn and admonish with wisdom.

One of the most important passages dealing with such loving confrontation is found in Galatians 6:1,2:

Brethren, if a man is overtaken in any trespass, you who are spiritual restore such a one in a spirit of gentleness, considering yourself lest you also be tempted. Bear one another's burdens, and so fulfill the law of Christ.

The *"law of Christ"* is the new commandment, the law of love. Love will seek to bear the burdens of others. It is not selfish; it cares what happens to other believers. It cannot sit idly by and watch another believer destroy his or her life.

The purpose of this confrontation is restoration, not condemnation. Too many times Christians are critical and judgmental of those who have fallen into sinful habits. The Bible warns those who confront to *"...consider yourself, lest you also be tempted."* We are all subject to the temptations of the enemy, and were it not for the sustaining grace of our Lord and the control of the Holy Spirit (Galatians 5:16), we would all be in a mess!

The person who admonishes, or confronts or warns needs to do it with "gentleness" or "meekness". That is the opposite of revenge or giving people what they really deserve. We need to have soft, tender hearts and truly desire to restore the erring brother or sister.

To love one another involves complete acceptance of all those who are true believers in Jesus Christ. It involves these five positive attitudes and actions that reveal our love for one another:

- An attitude of humility
- A commitment to integrity
- A willingness to forgive
- A dedication to ministry
- A desire to encourage

If these five qualities are seen in our lives, the world will know that we have been touched by the love of our Lord Jesus Christ and that we are truly His disciples!

Part Three

The Absence of Love

Chapter Three

The Absence of Love

Why Life Becomes Meaningless and Empty

Without love, life is a one-way street going nowhere! Without love, we feel alone and helpless. Without love, we turn to anger, hostility, bitterness and resentment. Without love, we lose our proper self-image and no longer regard our lives as meaningful and our activities as worthwhile.

Without love, people become self-destructive. Without love, people hurt, withdraw and run away. Without love, the alcoholic and the drug addict have no hope of recovery nor the will to get help. Without love, the child is afraid and insecure. Without love, the prospect of abuse grows stronger every day. Without love, sex loses its beauty and we become things to be used, abused and discarded. Without love, the marriage struggles and the family deteriorates.

Sometimes we're stubborn and selfish; it is sin that causes us to fail to experience God's love in our lives. That is a fundamental answer and it is important that we face it. My failure to love others with God's love is rooted in my sinful, selfish nature. Often I want to be loved before I am willing to give love to others.

Many people suffer from a family background that was not loving, and was, perhaps, even abusive. When parents do not love their children or display love between themselves, the children suffer. I have a little sign in my office that says, "The greatest thing a father can do for his children is to love their mother." In this day of easy and frequent divorce, these words are powerful.

When children who have not been loved by their parents become adults, they have already been programmed to be unloving parents, and they frequently reveal hostile behavior and lack the ability to relate in loving ways to others. Sometimes adults love in the wrong way because of past experiences that have not been wholesome and loving in the way God describes love in the Bible.

When discussing with one man his lack of affection for his children, he quickly answered with the example of his own parents. He had learned to avoid physical affection (demonstrating love) from his parents who never showed him that kind of affection. He felt that fathers who did that were not strong, and actually were spoiling their children. I felt sorry for him. His children were suffering because of his wrong beliefs.

Children learn much about love when they see it in the lives of their parents. Much of today's home life is saturated with argument, anger, bitterness, silence, withdrawal and ultimately, divorce. No wonder many people have difficulty in understanding and manifesting love in their relationships with others!

Some people are insecure in themselves due to past hurts and difficulties. It is hard for them to love because they are suspicious or are protective of themselves and their own family. They rarely reach out to other people and are afraid to love. After all, there is always a risk to take and a danger to face: What if the love is rejected or ignored? Can you remember how you felt when you tried to express a loving word or act to someone and he or she did not receive it well? Maybe he hurt you verbally, or just by his silence. If that happens to you often enough, you stop trying to love others. You withdraw and become insecure and very private.

Many of us have problems in loving because we set conditions. We love only if.... Sometimes that practice is learned in our childhood. When a parent says, "You do this and mother will love you," we grow up believing that there are conditions to be met before we can experience love. Often we feel that we can never measure up.

Many children believe that they are loved only when they do what meets with the approval of their parents, so they do things to please their parents in order to receive a measure of love. That practice often carries over into adult life: Adults dress a certain way in hopes of receiving the approval of others, they do constant acts of kindness and service in order to receive loving approval and response from others. When it doesn't come, the hurt gets deeper and it becomes more difficult for them to love in God's biblical way.

Some people find it difficult to love because of the way they have been used or abused in the past. One young girl who had great insecurity in her relationships with others had learned to withdraw and isolate herself because of the way she was treated. She was physically mature at an early age and became greatly enamored with the affection of boys. Having had little physical affection from her parents, she responded quickly to what the boys were giving her. One thing led to another and before long, she was "going all the way" with several boys. The word was out – she would do anything with anybody!

After a few weeks of these kinds of encounters, the boys dropped her. She was being used for sexual gratification and it finally got to her. As she got older, she became more suspicious and bitter, rarely showing any love to anyone, men in particular. Fortunately for her, through the godly counsel of an older woman, she learned about God's love and began to see her worth in the eyes of God. She started to build her life on right principles and today she is happily married with several children.

There is a fine line at times between love and hate, but there is a line! I have witnessed an enormous amount of hatred between married couples who supposedly loved each other. They become indignant when you suggest that there is a lack of love in their relationship. They fight, argue, shout at each other, kick, throw things and sometimes inflict bodily injury. Couples have been known to kill each other simply because of an argument or disagreement. When verbal or physical abuse occurs in a marriage, there is no way that God's love is controlling that marriage. Paul wrote:

Let all bitterness, wrath, anger, clamor, and evil
speaking be put away from you, with all malice.
And be kind to one another, tenderhearted,
forgiving one another, just as God in Christ also
forgave you (Ephesians 4:31,32).

It is difficult to love others if we set standards or
conditions that determine their worthiness to be loved. God
loves us as we are, knowing fully our weaknesses and sins.
When we are unlovely, He still loves us. His love is not
dependent upon our performance or worthiness. We often
have the "perfect person" in mind whom we would enjoy.
We see people in a certain light, and if they don't measure
up to this "perfect person", we don't express love to them.

I got excited one day at the office about having a
romantic date with my wife. I thought about what she
might wear and how she might respond. I stopped at the
florist and bought a single rosebud and put it in a lovely
vase. I bought a romantic card and made some great plans
for the evening – candlelight dinner, etc.

When I got home, I could just imagine how my wife was
going to respond. I even thought of how great it would be
if she met me at the door and threw her arms around me.
At the height of my anticipation, I opened the door, walked

in and said, "Honey, I'm home." No answer. I went upstairs and found her lying in bed, sick with the flu. Her hair was in curlers, she had no makeup on and she was wearing that old robe I don't like. Needless to say, my romantic ideas deteriorated rather rapidly! All of a sudden I didn't feel very "loving" anymore.

The Place to Start

If you want to know and experience God's love, and to see some changes in your present attitudes and actions, you're on the right track. Wanting to experience God's love is where it all begins. Many of us do not sense our need of His love, so we ignore our problems and neglect our responsibilities to love. Without God's love, life can become very meaningless, boring, lonely and empty.

I would like to suggest four simple steps that I believe could change your life and the lives of those around you whom you desire to love:

- Remember that we are sinful and selfish, and thus incapable of loving others the way God wants us to love them.

I know this may sound strange to you, but we have to begin here. Sometimes our pride stands in the way of our loving. We think there's nothing wrong with us and that with a little self-effort, we can love the way God wants us to love. Not a chance!

God's love is different from our natural responses and learned behavior patterns. His love is produced by the Holy Spirit, not by selfish effort and human motivation. It can be very liberating to admit selfishness, pride, anger, hostility, bitterness and resentment. Confession of what we are, say and do is the beginning of true healing and restoration.

He who covers his sins will not prosper, but whoever confesses and forsakes them will have mercy (Proverbs 28:13).

• Recognize that God's love is available only to believers in Jesus Christ, and that it is produced by the Holy Spirit of God.

You can never know the deep satisfaction of loving God's way until you first of all believe in Jesus Christ as your Lord and Savior from sin, death, and hell. He died on the cross, paying for your sins (past, present and future). Your sin was laid on Him and the Bible teaches that forgiveness (one of the great qualities of God's love) comes to you through faith in what Jesus Christ has already done. When He said on the cross, "It is finished!" it meant that nothing could be added to what He did. We can't earn our way into God's favor. We can't pay for it, and we (you and I) certainly don't deserve it! We must accept what Jesus Christ has already done for us at the cross 1900 years ago.

According to the Bible, Jesus Christ arose from the dead on the third day after His crucifixion.

If you confess with your mouth the Lord Jesus and believe in your heart that God has raised Him from the dead, you will be saved. For with the heart one believes to righteousness, and with the mouth confession is made to salvation (Romans 10:9,10).

"Believe on the Lord Jesus Christ, and you will be saved" (Acts 16:31).

When you decide to believe on the Lord Jesus Christ as your only Savior from sin, death and hell, God places His Holy Spirit within you. Christians speak of being "born again" by the work of the Holy Spirit. We become "new creatures in Christ" (II Corinthians 5: 17). Our bodies become the temple of the Holy Spirit of God, who is now in us (I Corinthians 6:19). Every believer has the Holy Spirit, but this doesn't mean that the Holy Spirit "has you" in the sense of controlling you. The Bible teaches that we need to be *"..filled with the Holy Spirit"* (Ephesians 5:18) and that we must *"...walk in the Spirit"* (Galatians 5:16) if we are going to have victory over sinful desires and habits and truly manifest God's love in our lives.

- Realize that our sinful and selfish natures need to be controlled.

This is a point at which many of us lose the battle. We begin to feel confident, that we can handle things ourselves. We ignore the Holy Spirit's ministry within us and even quench and grieve Him by our sinful, stubborn ways.

I say then: *Walk in the Spirit, and you shall not fulfill the lust of the flesh. For the flesh lusts against the Spirit, and the Spirit against the flesh; and these are contrary to one another, so that you do not do the things that you wish* (Galatians 5:16,17).

Christians can become quite frustrated in their attempts to love others if they do not rely upon the work of the Holy

Spirit within them. A failure to trust God can prove disastrous in our relationships with others.

To "walk in the Spirit" reveals a step-by-step, obedient lifestyle to what the Spirit wants you to do. The will of the Holy Spirit is revealed in God's Word, the Bible. The Holy Spirit is the real Author of the Bible (II Peter I:19-21), and if we are "walking in the Spirit" we are daily obeying what the Bible says.

• Respond to what the Bible says we should do, regardless of how we feel.

Many people do not experience God's love in their relationship with others because they depend too much upon their own feelings. That's dangerous! My feelings change constantly. They are sometimes affected by my health or physical condition. At other times, I feel things that are not true but simply the creations or fantasies of my own mind.

It is technically possible to love others even when you don't feel like it. Jesus said in John 14:15, *"If you love Me, keep My commandments."* Obedience is at the heart of God's love. I show love to another person when I obey the Bible's instruction about how to respond or not to respond. When I do what is right, I am demonstrating love. When I respond to mere feelings of so-called love, I often do the wrong thing and wind up violating God's Word.

One young man shared with me his strong feelings of love for a certain young lady. Unfortunately, these feelings led him to become involved with her sexually (they were not married). He reassured me that he really loved her or he would not feel as he did. I told him that although I understood how strong feelings of love could motivate a person to have sexual intercourse, according to the Bible this was not a demonstration of God's love. God's love, when it controls us, keeps us from having sexual intercourse until we are married. Instead of caring for her the way he should, protecting her from future emotional and physical problems that might result from the sexual involvement, he was controlled by his sexual desire and romantic feelings. We often sacrifice the permanent on the altar of the immediate.

That young man began to see that refraining from sexual intercourse before marriage was indeed an expression of God's love. His feelings did not change when he was with her, he still felt strong sexual desire for her, but now he was learning to express God's love by obeying God's Word (which forbids sexual intercourse before marriage) in spite of the way he felt. After a period of abstinence from the sexual activity, he and the girl of his dreams were married.

Does this mean that we will never have feelings of love for others when we love with God's love? Of course not. Feelings do come and they do exist, but they should not control what we do or do not do. When we are obedient to God's Word, proper feelings will result, and the ones we have will be controlled and refined by God.

The Love Chapter

I Corinthians 13 is the biblical description of God's love. It is located in a book that was written to a group of people who were really struggling. Verse 3 of chapter 3 describes them as "carnal". They were not walking in the Spirit. They had disagreements over speakers, were tolerating immorality (incest) in their membership, were confused about pagan practices and lifestyles, were confused about God's standards regarding marriage and divorce, were unloving toward fellow believers who disagreed with them on minor points of doctrine, were unsure of the Lord's teaching about the resurrection of the body and were hesitant about Christian giving.

The immediate context both before and after the love

chapter is the teaching about spiritual gifts. A list of gifts is given in I Corinthians 12 and an evaluation of the difference between the gift of speaking in tongues (foreign languages without previous knowledge) and the gift of prophecy (public proclamation of God's Word) is given in chapter 14. I Corinthians 14:1 begins with the words, *"Pursue love"* which (in this context) is an exhortation to an unloving group of people who were misusing their spiritual gifts and coveting gifts that the Holy Spirit had not given to some of them.

The Key Verse

> *Earnestly desire the best gifts. And yet I show you a more excellent way* (I Corinthians 12:31).

The previous two verses seem to imply that the Corinthians were confused about spiritual gifts. Could a person by his own desire and training use one of the gifts? Verse 11 of this chapter says, *"But one and the same Spirit works all these things, distributing to each one individually as He wills."* The spiritual gifts that God has given to each believer are given by the sovereign will of the Holy Spirit. Whatever gifts you have, you have. You cannot by prayer, fasting, pleading, study, experience, ability or any other human effort exercise a gift you do not have. If you try, it will be quickly evident to others that you are not gifted in what you are trying to do.

Paul writes to them in verses 28–30 of chapter 12:

God has appointed these in the church: first apostles, second prophets, third teachers, after that miracles, then gifts of healings, helps, administrations, varieties of tongues. Are all apostles? Are all prophets? Are all teachers? Are all workers of miracles? Do all have gifts of healings? Do all speak with tongues? Do all interpret?

These questions all require a negative answer in the grammar of the Greek language. "Do all?" Answer: Of course not! The Corinthians were evidently desiring the "best" or "greater" gifts, the ones that were more spectacular from a human point of view or that gave a person a measure of authority or that made other people believe that they were really important.

Verse 31 is either a command or a statement of fact; the Greek grammar allows for either one. Is Paul commending them for their attitudes toward spiritual gifts? Hardly. Why would he command them to desire something they could not have unless the Holy Spirit gave it to them? I Corinthians 14:1 says, *"Desire spiritual gifts",* but it does not say what I Corinthians 12:31 said, *"Desire the best [or greater] gifts."*

It would seem best to take the words *"...earnestly desire the best gifts"* as a simple statement of fact. Paul is stating that this is what the Corinthians were doing - desiring the best or greater gifts and as a result, they had become very unloving in their attitudes toward other believers with lesser gifts. They were missing *"...a more excellent way."*

The Corinthians were carnal, not spiritual. Paul is not commending them but seeking to correct their carnality and unloving ways. In today's culture of self-love promotion, one can easily see how the Corinthian problem can be duplicated in contemporary church life. When people are more interested in themselves than they are in loving others, carnality, division, strife, and disunity are always the result.

Behind the Corinthian problem lay a lack of doctrinal and theological understanding as well as a lack of contentment and peace about what God was doing. We need correct information about spiritual gifts and abilities that God has given. I Corinthians 4:7 says:

Who makes you differ from another? And what
do you have that you did not receive? Now if you
did indeed receive it, why do you glory as if you
had not received it?

Everything we are and have has come from the gracious hand of God. All the gifts, talents, and abilities that we have are sacred trusts from His hand, and *"...it is required in stewards that a man be found faithful"* (I Corinthians 4:1,2).

The Bible urges us to be content in all things, and it tells us that this contentment combined with godliness brings great gain (I Timothy 6:6-11). Carnal attitudes, on the other hand, become very destructive. Wanting things that God has never given us will produce great frustration and harm to ourselves and others. James 4:3 reminds us:

You ask and do not receive, because you ask
amiss, that you may spend it on your pleasures.

James warns us about *"bitter envy"* and *"self-seeking"* in our hearts (James 3:14). The Corinthians were desiring what God had not given, and were demonstrating a lack of love toward other members of the body.

The words, *"a more excellent way"*, emphasize that God's love is a continuing lifestyle, not simply a momentary act or a moment's feeling. It is a way of doing things, a habit of life. It is easy to think of love being expressed at a given point in time (and it often is!) but the more difficult understanding is that God's love is a way of life.

The words *"more excellent"* come from a Greek word which we use in English for an exaggeration: hyperbole. It refers to overstating a point for emphasis. The way of God's love needs to be exaggerated for emphasis. In one sense you cannot overstate the case about God's love, since it truly is the greatest thing: Nothing in life can equal it! God's love is obviously greater than all the gifts, and I Corinthians 13 will reveal why.

I Corinthians 14:1 begins with the words, *"Pursue love."* Where spiritual gifts have their proper place, the great priority in life for believers is to pursue God's love in all they do and say because without it life becomes meaningless and empty.

Paul's words in I Corinthians 12:31, *"And yet I show you"*, proves that God's love can be seen and understood. You can know this love of God; it is evident. A life that truly loves will be evident to everyone.

Three Paragraphs

I Corinthians 13 is composed of three paragraphs in Greek. Each paragraph reveals something about God's love.

- Paragraph 1 (I Corinthians 13:1-3)

It shows that God's love is necessary for all that we say and do and that without it, life becomes meaningless and empty.

- Paragraph 2 (I Corinthians 13:4-7)

It shows that God's love is different from natural human behavior.

- Paragraph 3 (I Corinthians 13:8-13)

It shows that God's love is greater than spiritual gifts and greater than faith and hope.

God's Love Is Necessary for All We Say and Do

Without God's love, life becomes meaningless and empty. I Corinthians 13:1-3 tells us why and insists that God's love is necessary for all we say and do.

Though I speak with the tongues of men and of angels, but have not love, I have become as sounding brass or a clanging cymbal.

And though I have the gift of prophecy, and understand all mysteries and all knowledge, and though I have all faith, so that I could remove mountains, but have not love, I am nothing.

And though I bestow all my goods to feed the poor, and though I give my body to be burned, but have not love, it profits me nothing.

One phrase is repeated three times in this first paragraph of the love chapter - *"but have not love...."* This repeated phrase makes it clear that there are three lines of thought in the paragraph (which the verse divisions reveal). This phrase also shows the possibility of using these gifts and doing these things without God's love.

The word, "though" (or "if"), which begins each verse suggests the thought that all of these examples are hypothetical. No one is exactly like these statements, but even if they were, without God's love the results are nothing! The points are exaggerated for emphasis so that none of us will miss the underlying theme: Without God's love our ministry is ineffective.

The conclusions in paragraph 1 are all different. Verse 1 says, *"I have become...."* This reveals what will happen to you without God's love. Verse two says, *"I am nothing".* This shows that a proper biblical self-image is based on God's love in your life. Verse 3 says, *"It profits me nothing".* By this, we understand what the results are when we give without love.

Three issues are dealt with in these three short and powerful verses: our personal communication, our spiritual understanding and our sacrificial giving. Without love, our communication is ineffective, our understanding is incomplete and our giving is insufficient.

Without God's Love Our Personal Communication is Ineffective

> *Though I speak with the tongues of men and angels, but have not love, I have become as sounding brass or a clanging cymbal.*

"Tongues" normally refers to languages. The word in Greek *(glossais)* appears 50 times in the New Testament in

its various forms. Even if you could speak in all the languages of the world known to mankind, without God's love, we are unimpressed. Linguistic ability is a wonderful talent and most valuable. World travel has brought people of different languages more closely together, but God's love is the best language of all; it communicates when mere eloquence can't.

The *"tongues of angels"* would be a more difficult skill than the *"tongues of men"*. What language do angels speak? When angels spoke to people in Bible times, it appears that they spoke in the language of the people they were talking to – Aramaic, Hebrew, Greek; it didn't seem to hold them back.

Some people say that the *"tongues of angels"* refer to heavenly language, and that the gift of tongues was that ability. Paul said that he was caught up to the third heaven or paradise (II Corinthians 12:2-4), where he heard *"...inexpressible words, which is not lawful for a man to utter."* The language of heaven was too difficult to repeat, and was not even allowed among humans!

Even if you could speak the *"tongues of angels"* (and in fact you cannot!), without God's love, the results are tragic. You have become as sounding brass or a clanging cymbal.

Beautiful language, wonderful eloquence, effective speaking – all are gifts from God but without His love, they are ineffective.

Love is the great need in communication. Several years ago, I was listening to a great speaker who was trying to impress his audience with his speaking ability, but there was little love in what he said. I thought then as I think now: Without love, real communication does not take place.

The words, *"I have become"*, indicate that the person's life was not always like this. He is responsible for this change. It is a simple reminder of how easy it is to slip from a Spirit-filled life of loving words to one that is mere noise and irritation to others.

These words also indicate that it is now a habit. How easy it is to develop a habit of speaking without love! You say all the right words, but something is missing – God's love.

One day, as I was trying desperately to get my point across to one of my children, I raised my voice and spoke with great authority. My child responded, "Do you love me, Daddy?" That hurt! Of course I love my child but at that moment, it was not coming through because of how I was speaking. My overall commitment is based on love for my child but on that occasion, the manner of my speaking was indicating the opposite.

Ephesians 4:15 urges us to *"speak the truth in love"*. That's a difficult assignment at times. Suppose a lady asked you what you thought of her new dress, and suppose it was really ugly. What would you tell her? Would you lie and say, "It's beautiful!" That's not biblical love. Would you say, "You look terrible in that; whatever made you buy it"? That doesn't sound too loving! To speak the truth in love requires some thought. Learn to compliment the person as well as to communicate the truth. Perhaps something like this would help: "For someone as attractive as you are, it doesn't do much for you!" Or, "I think that dress detracts from the good qualities you already have!" (If you don't like either of those responses, come up with your own!) In other words, show appreciation sincerely for the real person as well as communicating the truth as you see it.

"Sounding brass" and *"noisy gong"* refer to echoing brass. It indicates a constant and powerful repetition. One night at a church concert, I was sitting on the platform in front of the percussion section of the orchestra. Right in back of me was the person with the cymbals. When those cymbals came together, the sound wasn't too pleasant to my

ears! I kept hearing that echoing sound and it was not enjoyable. That's what it's like when you are speaking to someone without God's love – the sound hurts more than it helps!

A *"clanging cymbal"* is based on Greek words used for crying and weeping loudly over the dead. Somehow, that's the way it sounds when you try to communicate without love; it causes grief and sadness rather than joy.

Husbands are told in Colossians 3:19, *"Love your wives and do not be bitter toward them."* Literally this means, *"Stop being sharp toward your wives"*. The root word means "to cut" or "to prick". Speaking without love is like that. Many marriages are suffering because of bad communication on the part of the husband as well as the wife. There is a danger of not communicating with one another, but there is also a danger of communicating in the wrong way – without God's love!

When you love someone, you can say almost anything to him. Even when he doesn't agree with what you said, he still loves you for trying! I was going through that over the phone one day. The person I was talking with had unbelievable problems in his life. I cared about him but I just didn't have the answers he was seeking. He knew it and

I knew it. A few days later, he told me how much the conversation meant to him. He said, "You didn't have any answers, but I knew you cared about me and that was what I needed most at that time." (Not every situation works out like that. Sometimes I am unloving and uncaring, and I'm afraid it shows!)

Without God's Love, Our Spiritual Understanding is Incomplete

Though I have the gift of prophecy, and understand all mysteries and all knowledge, and though I have all faith, so that I could remove mountains, but have not love, I am nothing.

Spiritual understanding is a wonderful thing! Too many people are immature and even ignorant in their comprehension of spiritual and biblical truth. Yet spiritual understanding is not the highest good. It can even be deficient, though it is comprehensive. The missing ingredient may be love. Without God's love, your spiritual understanding is incomplete. That's the point behind verse 2.

The words, "*the gift of,*" are in italics which means that they are not found in the Greek text but are an interpretation of what is meant.

"*Prophecy*" refers to the content of God's revelation to man. In this sense, the whole Bible is prophecy. Peter spoke about this:

> *We also have the prophetic word made more sure, which you do well to heed as a light that shines in a dark place, until the day dawns and the morning star rises in your hearts; knowing this first, that no prophecy of Scripture is of any private interpretation, for prophecy never came by the will of man, but holy men of God spoke as they were moved by the Holy Spirit* (II Peter 1:19-21).

John said:

> *I testify to everyone who hears the words of the prophecy of this book: If anyone adds to these things, God will add to him the plagues that are written in this book; and if anyone takes away from the words of the Book of this prophecy, God shall take away his part from the Book of Life, from the Holy City, and from the things which are written in this book* (Revelation 22:19).

The Bible is prophecy, and is a completed revelation to which no one can add words and from which no one can take away words without suffering severe consequences.

The word, "prophecy", means "predicting the future" to most of us today, but that was not its primary meaning. The Greek form of the word simply means "to speak before" - not only speaking before an event occurred, but also speaking before a crowd of people. It refers to public speaking or proclamation. A "prophet" was a mouthpiece, speaking forth what he was told. The gift of prophesying was obviously very important in the early church. I Corinthians 14:3 says, *"He who prophesies speaks edification and exhortation and comfort to men."* Verse 4 says, *"He who prophesies edifies the church."*

However, even if you have the gift of proclaiming God's truth but you don't have God's love, the Bible says you are nothing - a big zero! Your worth is at an all-time low when you don't have God's love.

The phrase, *"...understand all mysteries and all knowledge",* is certainly comprehensive. *"All"* indicates that this person has really arrived in terms of spiritual understanding. The *"mysteries"* refer to everything that God has kept as a secret in the past, waiting for the proper time to reveal them. *"All knowledge"*, of course, refers to everything there is to know. Specifically, the point probably refers to all that God wants us to know. Even if this were possible, without God's love in your life, you are nothing.

No verse disturbs the Christian scholar and student like this one. There are so few believers who really study as they should. When one comes along who is a real student of the Word, it is refreshing to see. People will flock to hear someone like that who really knows what he is talking about, but without God's love, he is nothing. That's hard to accept, but it is true.

I Corinthians 8:1 says, *"Knowledge puffs up, but love edifies."* Knowledge can make a person arrogant, but God's love seeks to build up others. Believers are encouraged and edified in the sphere of God's love (Ephesians 4:15,16).

God puts no premium on ignorance, but He doesn't honor knowledge without love, either. The formula should be "Knowledge + Love." They go together; both are needed. However, the most important, and truly the greatest, is God's love.

What About Removing Mountains?

"Removing mountains" is no small task! It takes great faith, we are told. What kind of faith is under discussion here? It is a bit difficult to be dogmatic, but here are a few considerations.

- The concept of faith removing mountains is used in Matthew 17:20.

Jesus said to them, *"...because of your unbelief; for assuredly I say to you, if you have faith as a mustard seed, you will say to this mountain, 'move from here to there,' and it will move; and nothing will be impossible for you."*

The problem in this passage was the inability of the disciples to cast out a demon from an epileptic boy. Jesus said that they lacked faith.

There is a spiritual gift mentioned in I Corinthians 12:9 called *"faith"*. Could this be the ability to cast out demons? In Mark 16:17,18, Jesus mentioned some miraculous things that the apostles would be able to do. One of them was to *"...cast out demons"*. Since He mentioned that they would *"...speak with new tongues"* (one of the gifts of I Corinthians 12), could it not be possible that the ability to cast out demons was also one of the spiritual gifts - namely, faith?

- Another usage of faith removing mountains is
  found in Matthew 21:21,22.

*Jesus answered and said to them, "Assuredly I
say to you, if you have faith and do not doubt,
you will not only do what was done to the fig
tree, but also if you say to this mountain, 'Be
removed and be cast into the sea,' it will be done.
And all things, whatever you ask in prayer,
believing, you will receive."*

The background here was the ability of Jesus to cause a
fig tree to wither by simply speaking a word of
condemnation to it for not having figs, but only leaves.

- Without faith we cannot please God, according
  to Hebrews 11:6.

There is a sense in which all believers must have faith,
even though not all believers have the specific spiritual gift
of faith. Believers must have faith when they become
believers, and they must also apply faith in their Christian
lives. Ephesians 2:8 says, *"By grace you have been saved,
through faith."* Colossians 2:6 says, *"As you have therefore
received Christ Jesus the Lord, so walk in Him."* We become
Christians by faith and we live our Christian lives by faith.

- Faith is the ability to trust God in difficult circumstances, according to Hebrews 11:32-40:

"All these, having obtained a good testimony through faith, did not receive the promise, God having provided something better for us, that they should not be made perfect apart from us."

The long list of names in these verses reveals the difficult circumstances through which believers in the past have gone. They have suffered greatly and many were killed for their faith. The faith of this passage is the ability to trust God in difficult circumstances and all believers are enjoined to have this kind of faith (as well as saving faith and the trusting faith of daily Christian living).

Faith that removes mountains seems to be of a more miraculous nature than other kinds of faith. Whether it is the ability to cast out demons or to cause a fig tree to wither, we do not know. It might apply to many kinds of situations. The point of I Corinthians 13:2 is that even if you had "all" faith that any person could possibly display in his life, but you did not have God's love, you are nothing.

Prophecy, mysteries, knowledge, faith- all wonderful

gifts; yet, without God's love you are nothing, though you have them all. This reveals what is really wrong with a person who claims to have great spiritual understanding but who rarely affects people in a positive, encouraging way. People couldn't care less about what this person knows because they see little evidence of love in his life.

It's easy to be satisfied with spiritual knowledge. It's rather simple to be confident that you are on the right track when you have so much knowledge. But being right all the time on every issue does not mean that you have a ministry in the lives of others. Without love, there are few results.

I had a friend like that. He was usually right on every issue. He loved to study and to learn new truths. He talked about knowing the truth and making sure of what the Bible said in every single passage. That is, of course, an important thing. What is true is not what I think, but what God's Word says. Somehow, however, people did not respond to this person and he felt very lonely. When he talked, people got bored and turned him off. He wanted to tell others what he knew, and he knew plenty, but his problem was that he did not love. People could feel that and it was hard for them to listen to him because of it. I have seen that problem in many people, including myself. I love to study and to learn; I always have, but one thing I still need to learn is how to love people with God's love.

Don't misunderstand what has been said – knowledge and spiritual understanding are very important. Don't excuse yourself by saying that since knowledge without love is not effective, you won't bother learning anymore! We must continue to learn and grow mentally but in the process, we must also learn more of God's love. Our own biblical sense of self-image is related to this fact. The phrase, "I am nothing", indicates the real truth – God's love establishes your worth for He loves us when we are unlovely. Our love for others also builds them up, for nothing is so encouraging or up-building than to experience the love of God through another believer's life and ministry.

Without Love Your Sacrificial Giving is Insufficient

Though I bestow all my goods to feed the poor,
and though I give my body to be burned, but
have not love, it profits me nothing.

This is philanthropy at its best. Talk about "social consciousness"! Here is evidence of human concern for the poor of this world, but without God's love, there is no profit in God's eyes. Without God's love, your sacrificial giving is insufficient and it does not produce proper results. The words "the poor" are in italics, meaning that they are not in the Greek Text. The verb "to feed" literally means "to feed by little bits". It is used of feeding children and young animals. In modern Greek, the word refers to "bread" and the verb means "to shop".

Spiros Zodhiates in his wonderful book, *To Love Is To Live*, makes this statement:

It does not follow that the more we give away the more we shall love God but rather that the more we love God, the more we shall be willing to give away. What we do is always the result of what we are. To give because we believe that in this way we shall enjoy more of God's blessing and God Himself, is loveless charity.

II Corinthians 8:5 states that the Macedonian believers (poor financially, but rich spiritually) demonstrated the real priority in all Christian giving. They "...*first gave themselves to the Lord*".

To give *"all my goods"* suggests a tremendous commitment. Most of us give only a portion of our income. Frequently, what we give is so small that we don't sense any real sacrifice at all. To give everything away shows a great deal of dedication but without God's love, there is no profit in it. That's difficult to believe but that's what God's Word says. You can give without love but you cannot love without giving! Don't stop giving, but start loving!

I thought about the importance of love one day when a little child in our church sent me a note which said, "I love you, Pastor, and here's a quarter – take your family out to lunch!" That quarter was special to me. It wasn't nearly enough to pay for lunch but I didn't care – the thought behind it was worth much more than the amount.

The poor widow of Luke 21:1-4 gave two small copper coins, and it didn't seem like much in comparison to all the rest putting their gifts into the temple treasury. But Jesus said, *"Truly I say to you that this poor widow has put in more than all; for all these out of their abundance have put in offerings for God, but she out of her poverty has put in all the livelihood that she had."*

The phrase, *"Though I give my body to be burned"*, is based on late readings of the manuscript evidence available on this passage. Earlier readings contain the words *"that I might boast"*. The difference between "burned" and "boast" is only one letter in Greek. Copyists could easily have made this mistake. The oldest manuscripts (not necessarily the best) contain the reading *"to boast"*.

The statement could be referring to the giving of oneself, as a slave would do by necessity. In this case, you would give yourself out of choice, not compulsion. Paul spoke of giving (or presenting) your body to God for His service (Romans 12:1).

Some see this statement as referring to the act of martyrdom. They rely on the manuscript evidence that indicates "burned" instead of "boast". However, it seems to me that the words, *"that I might boast"*, fit better in the context.

Many of us have the ability to make great dedications and sacrifices. We can give ourselves to great causes, but often the motive is selfish - we are "boasting". We take great pride in our commitment, but that's not the way God's love works.

Matthew 6:1-4 warns us about doing things to be seen by others. Our commitment to give is to be in secret. Our heavenly Father, who sees in secret, will reward us in His own time and in His own way.

In examining this verse about sacrificial giving, it seems that two things are revealed: First, your purpose in giving reveals whether there is love or not – *"that I might boast"*. If your purpose is to brag about how great a person you are because of what you have done, then you lack God's love in your life.

Second, the profit you receive in giving is not found in what was given (as to amount of cost) but in the motive behind it – love! We tend to pay too much attention to the size of the gift rather than the motive behind the gift. The great profit is not found in the size but in the reason.

In today's culture, the size of the gift becomes increasingly important to people, but God is not broke. Costs may escalate but God's method of evaluation remains the same. The Lord is more interested in your motives than in your amounts. Many of us give because we want to receive and that too reveals the lack of love in our hearts.

What's wrong with sacrificial giving? Nothing, if there is love behind it; everything, if there is no love. John 3:16 reminds us that:

"God so loved the world that He gave His only begotten Son, that whoever believes in Him should not perish but have everlasting life."

John 15:13 says,

"Greater love has no one than this, than to lay down one's life for his friends."

By this we know love, because He laid down His life for us. And we also ought to lay down our lives for the brethren. But whoever has this world's goods, and sees his brother in need, and shuts up his heart from him, how does the love of God abide in him? My little children, let us not love in word or in tongue, but in deed and in truth (I John 3:16-18).

God's love will actually give and not just mouth the words. God's love will make great sacrifices for the benefit of the object loved, but it is impossible to give and make great sacrifices without having any love in your heart. There is no substitute for God's love – it is truly our greatest need!

Part Four

The Response of Love

How Love Treats Others

Chapter Four

The Response of Love

Love Suffers Long

Love focuses on people and is patient or longsuffering. "God is love," says I John 4:8, so it is not surprising to learn that one of God's marvelous attributes is patience or longsuffering.

A Brief Analysis of I Corinthians 13:4-7

Before we plunge into a discussion about how love responds to people, we need to analyze the second paragraph of I Corinthians 13, since it is the heart of the description of God's love. These verses are a gold mine of information on love but, as with most of God's blessings, they must be applied and that's not so easy to do.

- Love suffers long and is kind;
- Love does not envy;
- Love does not parade itself,
- Is not puffed up;
- Does not behave rudely,

- Does not seek its own,
- Is not provoked,
- Thinks no evil;
- Does not rejoice in iniquity, but
- Rejoices in the truth;
- Bears all things,
- Believes all things,
- Hopes all things,
- Endures all things.

The word "love" is actually used only twice in this paragraph, although the English translation uses it four times. "Love" appears before the words "suffers long" and the word "kind". In each case, the definite article is in front of the word "love". God's love is summarized in the first two qualities – longsuffering and kindness. Everything else that is said describes those two qualities in action.

After stating what God's love is (two positives), the text then tells us what love is not (eight negatives). We often learn best what something is by knowing what it is not.

Verse 7 makes four statements about God's love as it relates to "all things". This verse tells us how God's love reacts to all the changing circumstances and situations that we inevitably face in life.

There are only 41 words in Greek that comprise this beautiful description of God's love (56 words in English). All of the verbs (15 of them in Greek) are in the present tense, a tense which indicates a continual habit of life. God's love truly is a way of life! In fact, I Corinthians 12:31 calls it "...a more excellent way".

The first two positive descriptions (patience and longsuffering) show how God's love is different from natural human behavior in the way it interacts with people. The eight negatives reveal that God's love does not act with selfish attitudes. The final four statements about "all things" reveal how God's love is different in its reaction to changing circumstances.

God's Love Is Longsuffering

As mentioned above, the definite article appears in the text of I Corinthians 13:4 in front of the word "love". It reads literally, "The love suffers long" and refers to the particular love that comes only from God. The only time the word "love" appears in this paragraph is with the opening two positive qualities – longsuffering and kindness. This proves that these two qualities summarize God's love. When you have these two operating in your life as habits, then you are loving the way God intends you to love.

If there is one quality above all others which people seem to have trouble with, it is patience or longsuffering. The Greek word means "taking a long time to boil". It is always used with respect to persons, not things or situations. There is also a Greek word meaning patience toward things and circumstances, and it is found in I Corinthians 13:7, but here in verse 4 we are talking about patience toward people.

God is never said to be patient toward things. He doesn't need that kind of patience for He controls all things. The Bible does teach, however, that God is patient toward people. II Peter 3:9 says that the Lord *"...is longsuffering toward us, not willing that any should perish but that all should come to repentance."*

Longsuffering is a fruit of the Holy Spirit, mentioned in Galatians 5:22. It is not natural to exhibit this kind of patience; it requires divine help. Instead, it is natural to be quite impatient with the way people act.

I found myself quite upset one day with the way a certain person was doing a job I had asked him to do. I was very impatient with him because of his attitude and the speed at which he was doing this task since it was not the speed I expected or demanded. But then I began to feel sick inside when I realized that my impatience was getting the best of me. When I sought God's help and confessed my sin, I noticed an immediate change in my attitude. The speed of that person no longer mattered; I was now happy that he was involved in helping me.

Needing God's help and admitting that you can't handle things is a first step to having patience. I Thessalonians 5:14 says that we are to be *"patient with all"*, even though not everyone meets our standards or demands for deserving our patience.

The concept of patience toward people is perhaps best understood by the word, "longsuffering", which is frequently described as one who is "slow to anger". The Greek word *(makrothumeo* or *makrothumia* or *makrothumos)* is used 25 times in the New Testament. (In the Old Testament, the quality of being "slow to anger" is frequently translated in the Greek version of the Hebrew language with the word *makrothumia,* or "longsuffering.")

The Longsuffering of God

God had longsuffering while Noah was building the ark:

*Who formerly were disobedient, when once the
long suffering of God waited in the days of
Noah, while the ark was being prepared, in
which a few, that is, eight souls, were saved
through the water* (I Peter 3:20).

The story reveals a wicked generation and regret on the
part of God in creating man:

*Then the Lord saw that the wickedness of man
was great in the earth, and that every intent of
the thoughts of his heart was only evil
continually. And the Lord was sorry that He had
made man on the earth, and He was grieved in
His heart* (Genesis 6:5,6).

Expressing His great longsuffering toward the
wickedness and rebellion of planet Earth, the Bible says;

*My Spirit shall not strive with man forever, for
he is indeed flesh; yet his days shall be one
hundred and twenty years* (Genesis 6:3).

Longsuffering does not mean that judgment is ignored
or man's sin overlooked; it is a word referring to time. God
gives us time to reconsider and repent because He is

longsuffering. After 120 years of preaching by Noah during which the ark was being built, God finally brought His judgment of a worldwide flood upon the earth, destroying the entire first civilization of millions of people with the exception of Noah, his sons, and their wives.

God takes a long time to boil (for which most of us are indeed thankful!) and the root reason behind His incredible patience toward undeserving, rebellious people is His great love. Yes, love is patient and suffers long!

In a marvelous discussion about the sovereignty of God, Romans 9:18-24 reveals the longsuffering of God toward unbelievers:

> *Therefore He has mercy on whom He wills, and whom He wills He hardens. You will say to me then, "Why does He still find fault? For who has resisted His will?" But indeed, O man, who are you to reply against God? Will the thing formed say to him who formed it, "Why have you made me like this?" Does not the potter have power over the clay, from the same lump to make one vessel for honor and another for dishonor? What if God, wanting to show His wrath and to make His power known, endured with much*

longsuffering the vessels of wrath prepared for
destruction, and that He might make known the
riches of His glory on the vessels of mercy,
which He had prepared beforehand for glory,
even us whom He called, not of the Jews only,
but also of the Gentiles?

God *"endured with much longsuffering the vessels of*
wrath prepared for destruction." He endures the
disobedience, rebellion, and sin of unbelievers.

When God proclaimed His name to Moses, he referred
to His character and attributes as reflecting longsuffering:

Then the Lord descended in the cloud and stood
with him there, and proclaimed the name of the
Lord. And the Lord passed before him and
proclaimed, "The Lord, the Lord God, merciful
and gracious, longsuffering, and abounding in
goodness and truth, keeping mercy for
thousands, forgiving iniquity and transgression
and sin, by no means clearing the guilty, visiting
the iniquity of the fathers upon the children and
the children's children to the third and fourth
generation" (Exodus 34:5-7).

Moses prayed this remarkable prayer:

The Lord is longsuffering and abundant in mercy, forgiving iniquity and transgression, but He by no means clears the guilty, visiting the iniquity of the fathers on the children to the third and fourth generation. Pardon the iniquity of this people, I pray, according to the greatness of Your mercy, just as You have forgiven this people from Egypt and even until now (Numbers 14:18,19).

The longsuffering of God is associated with the qualities of mercy, grace and forgiveness.

In the Psalms, we have these qualities blended together once more, along with the mention of "slow to anger" or the "longsuffering" of God.

The Lord is merciful and gracious, slow to anger, and abounding in mercy. He will not always strive with us, nor will He keep his anger forever. He has not dealt with us according to our sins, nor punished us according to our iniquities. For as the heavens are high above the earth, so great is His mercy toward those who fear Him; as far as the east is from the west, so far has He removed our transgressions from us. As a father pities his children, so the Lord pities those who fear Him. For He knows our frame; He remembers that we are dust (Psalm 103:8–14).

How wonderful is the longsuffering of God! It is so often associated with God's mercy, holding back from us what we really deserve. Behind all of this is the fact that God is love – the dominant attribute and essential character of God Himself. All that He plans, says and does is governed by His great love and it flows with mercy and longsuffering to both unbelievers and believers.

You, O Lord, are a God full of compassion, and gracious, longsuffering and abundant in mercy and truth (Psalm 86:15).

Compassion, grace, mercy – these are commonly associated with longsuffering. These are powerful descriptions of the nature of our God, Who is all-loving and demonstrates it in all His ways and doings.

The Characteristics of Longsuffering

Since the love of God is described as being the love that suffers long or is patient toward people, and is the result of the Holy Spirit producing His fruit in our lives, what characteristics of this love can we expect to see in our dealings with people?

- **You are slow to anger**. That's what the words mean – "taking a long time to boil" or to get angry. When God's love is controlling you, you are longsuffering; you don't "fly off the handle" and get angry easily. You take time to think about the difficult situation and respond to it in love.

Several factors are evident when you are slow to get angry.

You have great understanding. Proverbs 14:29 says, *"He who is slow to wrath has great understanding, but he who is impulsive exalts folly."* We do not manifest the wisdom of God but rather, we reveal that we are foolish when we get angry quickly and impulsively.

You avoid hostile arguments. Proverbs 15:18 says, *"A wrathful man stirs up strife, but he who is slow to anger allays contention."* The quickest way to explode a difficult, tense disagreement into an angry, hostile argument is to get immediately angry because someone disagrees with you.

You control your own spirit. Proverbs 16:32 teaches, *"He who is slow to anger is better than the mighty, and he who rules his spirit than he who takes a city."* We might have a tendency to honor the military conqueror, but God honors the person who controls his or her own spirit. That battle is often more difficult than any military conflict!

You overlook transgressions against you. Proverbs 19:11 says, *"The discretion of man makes him slow to anger, and it is to his glory to overlook a transgression. Love covers all sins"* (Proverbs 10:12). We can easily be stirred to angry responses when someone deliberately attacks us or sins against us. Longsuffering takes time, thinks about it, and is willing to overlook the offense and move on.

- **You are merciful and compassionate.** The second major characteristic of longsuffering is obvious from the descriptions used of God's longsuffering. God is merciful and compassionate; He does not deal with our sins with strict justice in every case. His longsuffering softens what we deserve, holds it back and gives us another chance.

The apostle Paul saw this characteristic of God's longsuffering in his own life. He writes his own personal testimony:

I thank Christ Jesus our Lord, Who has enabled me, because He counted me faithful, putting me into the ministry, although I was formerly a blasphemer, a persecutor, and an insolent man; but I obtained mercy because I did it ignorantly in unbelief. And the grace of our Lord was exceedingly abundant, with faith and love which are in Christ Jesus. This is a faithful saying and worthy of all acceptance, that Christ Jesus came into the world to save sinners, of whom I am chief. However, for this reason I obtained mercy, that in me first Jesus Christ might show all longsuffering, as a pattern to those who are going to believe on Him for everlasting life. Now to the King eternal, immortal, invisible, to God Who alone is wise, be honor and glory forever and ever. Amen (I Timothy 1:12–17).

Paul speaks of the abundant grace and mercy of God
that was extended toward him in spite of his depravity and
sinful rebellion. He says that Jesus Christ revealed in His life
and example the attribute of longsuffering. What a
wonderful attitude toward the marvelous love of God!

Mercy and compassion understands sin and depravity
and is not surprised at the failure and sinful ways of men
and women. It identifies with the vulnerability and
struggles of others and is willing to be patient.

- **You are willing to forgive**. As God described
  His own name and character in Exodus 34,
  referring to His longsuffering, He proclaimed
  that the heart of His nature and actions toward
  us is that of forgiveness - "forgive iniquity"
  (v.7).

In Isaiah, we learn that God's forgiving ways are totally
different from the way man would operate:

*Seek the Lord while He may be found, call upon
Him while He is near. Let the wicked forsake his
way, and the unrighteous man his thoughts; let
him return to the Lord, and He will have mercy
on him; and to our God for He will abundantly*

pardon. "For my thoughts are not your thoughts,
nor are your ways My ways," says the Lord. "For
as the heavens are higher than the earth, so are
My ways higher than your ways, and My
thoughts than your thoughts" (Isaiah 55: 6-9).

God will have mercy and abundantly pardon. Why? Because His ways are not our ways, and His thoughts are not our thoughts. How wonderful is the love of God! God is willing to forgive us when we do not deserve it and have done nothing in our performance or attitudes to prove that we are worthy of His forgiveness.

Jesus told a story of forgiveness connected with longsuffering in Matthew 18:21-35. Peter wanted to know how often we should forgive our brother who sins against us, and he suggested seven times. The Lord, however, replied with, "Seventy times seven" or, to put it another way, with no limitation whatsoever.

Jesus then told a story about a king who wanted to settle accounts with his slaves. One owed him ten talents and did not have the means to repay. The king ordered him to be sold, along with his wife and children and all that he had. Then, according to Matthew 18:26, the slave fell down before the king and said, *"Have patience with me, and I will pay you all."* The king then felt compassion and forgave him.

Later the slave went to a fellow-slave who owed him
only a hundred *denarii.* His fellow-slave fell down before
him and begged him saying, *"Have patience with me, and I
will pay you all."* But the slave was not compassionate like
his king, but threw his fellow-slave in prison until he paid
him what was owed.

When the king heard of it, he was angry and handed
the first slave over to the torturers until he repaid his debt.
Jesus commented on the whole incident with these words
in verse 35:

*So My heavenly Father also will do to you if each
of you from his heart does not forgive his
brother his trespasses.*

- **You are willing to endure the faults and
  weaknesses of others**. The word used with
  longsuffering that describes this trait is
  forbearance or "bearing with one another". It
  literally means to put up with others when
  they are not pleasant or have failed to do
  what you expected or do not respond as you
  would desire or think appropriate. There are
  many difficult people in the world.
  Longsuffering is definitely needed in order to
  endure the unattractive attitudes and actions
  of people.

Ephesians 4:2 says, *"With longsuffering, bearing with one another in love."* Here the motive is to keep the unity of the Spirit among believers (v.3). Colossians 3:12,13 agrees when it speaks of the qualities we need in our relationships with others and speaks of longsuffering – *"...bearing with one another, and forgiving one another".*

Forbearance is placed with longsuffering and goodness in describing how God through His goodness will lead us to repentance (Romans 2:4). God draws us with His love, even when we need to be hit over the head for what we have done and said! Peter spoke of *"the longsuffering of our Lord"* and said that it *"is salvation"* (II Peter 3:15). Earlier in the chapter (II Peter 3:9), he referred to God's *"...longsuffering toward us, not willing that any should perish but that all should come to repentance."*

- **You are willing to listen.** This is a simple application, but a practical demonstration that God's love is controlling you. An exciting story told with great enthusiasm might capture our attention for a moment but in normal conversation, one of the most effective skills of communication is lacking in most of us – the ability to listen, and to listen well with an understanding and sympathetic heart.

In Acts 26:3, the apostle Paul was standing before King Agrippa and said, *"Especially because you are expert in all customs and questions which have to do with the Jews; therefore, I beg you to hear me patiently."* Paul simply wanted him to listen to his defense. Listening to others is often a manifestation of God's love. It is willing to listen even when it is not convenient, interesting or particularly enjoyable.

God's love is primarily characterized by longsuffering and patience toward people. If longsuffering is being demonstrated in your life, the following things are true of you:

- You are slow to anger.
- You are merciful and compassionate.
- You are willing to forgive.
- You are willing to endure the faults and weaknesses of others.
- You are willing to listen.

Is God's love, the love that suffers long, controlling your life and bringing blessings to others?

Love Is Kind

One of the most beautiful qualities of spiritual love is that of kindness. Kindness is the opposite of attack, harshness or insensitivity to human need. Kindness wants to help and be a blessing more than a burden or hardship.

Kindness was a friend who, upon hearing that my car was in the garage, offered me one of his two cars to drive as long as I needed it. Kindness was the way an elderly lady told me that the way I spoke to another person was not good. She did it in private and started with words of love, support and encouragement. She was protective but not demanding. She cared because she loved me and wanted me to be effective with others at all times.

Kindness came when a dear friend who knew of my hurt and disappointment prayed in my presence for God's comfort, wisdom and peace. The immediate result was a calm and a deep awareness that all would be well. Kindness is a warm smile when there is pressure, disagreement and potential harm to human relationships. Kindness is a note saying that you were missed.

Biblical Usage

Two words summarize the love of God - longsuffering

and kindness. The words "THE love" appear before both of these verb forms. *"THE love suffers long"* and, *"THE love is kind."* The present tense in Greek indicates that these are habits of life, continuing lifestyles. God's love continues to suffer long and God's love is continually kind.

Forms of the Greek word for "kind" appear 19 times in the New Testament. Sometimes the word is translated "goodness". The basic meaning of the word is "useful, serviceable, adapted to its purpose", and often "excellent or valuable" as a result of its usefulness. When referring to foods, it can mean that which is healthful or tasty. I like to think that God's love is both good for you (healthful) and delicious to the taste!

The word "kind" or "kindness" in the Old Testament reflects several Hebrew words. The older counselors of Rehoboam (II Chronicles 10:7) exhorted him, *"If you are kind to these people, and please them, and speak good words to them, they will be your servants forever."* The word translated "kind" is the common Hebrew word for "good" *(tov)*.

In Genesis 24:49 the servant of Abraham said, *"If you will deal kindly and truly with my master, tell me."* The word comes from a beautiful and rich Hebrew word *(chesed)* which is often translated "lovingkindness" or "mercies". It is the major word for "kindness" in the Hebrew Old Testament and is translated that way in about 45 places in the English Bible.

Our Loving God Is Kind

Nehemiah 9:17 describes the character of God:

You are God, ready to pardon, gracious and merciful, slow to anger, abundant in kindness, and did not forsake them.

Psalm 63:3 says, *"Your lovingkindness is better than life."* The psalmist declares:

I will worship toward Your holy temple, and praise Your name for Your lovingkindness and Your truth; for You have magnified Your word above all Your name (Psalm 138:2).

Romans 2:4 refers to the riches of God's kindness:

Do you despise the riches of His goodness, forbearance, and longsuffering, not knowing that the goodness of God leads you to repentance?

The second word "goodness" in the Greek language is the same word translated "kind" in the love chapter, I Corinthians 13:4. God's lovingkindness leads us to repentance – what a beautiful and powerful thought!

Luke 6:35 says that God is "...*kind to the unthankful and evil*". I Peter 2:3 says that "...*the Lord is gracious*". The word "gracious" is the same word "kind". Ephesians 2:7 says concerning God's grace in salvation:

That in the ages to come He might show the exceeding riches of His grace in His kindness toward us in Christ Jesus.

Titus 3:4 speaks of the "...*kindness and the love of God our Savior*". The very next verse tells us that salvation is not the result of our works of righteousness but is rooted in God's mercy. It is the kindness of God that saves, not our own deeds.

Therefore consider the goodness and severity of God: on those who fell, severity; but toward you, goodness, if you continue in His goodness. Otherwise you also will be cut off (Romans 11:22).

The salvation of the Gentiles is made possible by the "goodness" (Greek word for "kindness") of God.

When you examine the use of the word translated "lovingkindness" as it relates to our loving God, it reveals the depth of His love in relating to us, sinful creatures that we are. Consider the following passages from the Psalms which use the word:

Show Your marvelous lovingkindness by Your right hand, O You Who save those who trust in You (Psalm 17:7).

Your lovingkindness is before my eyes (Psalm 26:3).

How precious is Your lovingkindness, O God! Therefore the children of men put their trust under the shadow of Your wings (Psalms 36:7).

Do not withhold Your tender mercies from me, O Lord; let Your lovingkindness and Your truth continually preserve me (Psalm 40:11).

The Lord will command His lovingkindness in the daytime, and in the night His song shall be with me – a prayer to the God of my life (Psalm 42:8).

We have thought, O God, on Your lovingkindness, in the midst of Your temple (Psalm 48:9).

Have mercy upon me, O God, according to Your lovingkindness, according to the multitude of Your tender mercies, blot out my transgressions (Psalm 51:1).

Hear me, O Lord, for Your lovingkindness is good; Turn to me according to the multitude of Your tender mercies (Psalm 69:16).

Whoever is wise will observe these things, and they will understand the lovingkindness of the Lord (Psalm 107:43).

Revive me according to your lovingkindness, so that I may keep the testimony of Your mouth (Psalm 119:88).

Hear my voice according to Your lovingkindness; O Lord, revive me according to Your justice (Psalm 119:149).

Cause me to hear Your lovingkindness in the morning, for in You do I trust (Psalm 143:8).

The Lord said:

I have loved you with an everlasting love; therefore with lovingkindness I have drawn you (Jeremiah 31:3).

God's lovingkindness is a clear demonstration of His great love toward us.

What Kindness Does

Kindness responds as God would respond. Kindness is a fundamental characteristic (along with longsuffering) of God's love. It reflects a concern for others and desires to help. It does not ignore, neglect or withdraw. It does whatever can be done to bless the life of another person.

- **It shows compassion for the needs of others**. Here is a fascinating look into the meaning of kindness:

It came to pass in the thirty-seventh year of the captivity of Jehoiachin king of Judah, in the

*twelfth month, on the twenty-fifth day of the
month, that Evil-Merodach king of Babylon, in
the first year of his reign, lifted up the head of
Jehoiachin king of Judah and brought him out
of prison. And he spoke kindly to him and gave
him a more prominent seat than those of the
kings who were with him in Babylon. So
Jehoiachin changed his prison garments, and he
ate bread regularly before the king all the days
of his life. And as for his provisions, there was a
regular ration given him by the king of Babylon,
a portion for each day until the day of his death,
all the days of his life* (Jeremiah 52:31-34).

Evil-Merodach, king of Babylon, showed kindness to
Jehoiachin, king of Judah, by bringing him out of prison
and exalting him. Verse 32 says that he "spoke kindly" to
him and set his throne above the thrones of the kings who
were with him in Babylon. Verse 33 says that Jehoiachin
had his meals with the king all the days of his life, and that
a regular allowance was given to him until the day of his
death (verse 34). That's what I call kindness!

When you are kind, you have compassion for others
who are in need and you do something about it! What you
do should be useful to them. Only then is God's love
operating, and only then are you really kind.

Have you ever received a gift from someone that was really intended for them, not you? It was in no way useful to you but rather for someone else. Was true love shown to you? God's love is concerned about doing what is useful for the object of that love because it is kind.

God's lovingkindness is usually connected with His tender mercies or compassion. He knows what we are like, and understands our weakness and vulnerability. He acts in kindness, remembering that we are but dust (Psalm 103:13, 14).

- **It desires to forgive.** Paul wrote in Ephesians 4:32, *"Be kind to one another, tenderhearted, forgiving one another, just as God in Christ also forgave you."* The word for "forgiving" and "forgave" is the Greek word translated "grace". Grace extends to us what we do not deserve. Kindness desires to forgive, giving to others what they do not deserve, but that which kindness must give.

Paul wrote these words:

Therefore, as the elect of God, holy and beloved, put on tender mercies, kindness, humbleness of mind, meekness, longsuffering; bearing with one another, and forgiving one another, if anyone has a complaint against another; even as Christ forgave you, so you also must do (Colossians 3:12,13).

Kindness is one of the qualities that we need as believers in order to exercise forgiveness to one another as Jesus Christ has done for us.

- **It does good to those who are enemies and those who are not thankful, but evil.** A wonderful text about kindness is found in the teaching of our Lord Jesus Christ. It deals with loving our enemies:

But I say to you who hear: Love your enemies, do good to those who hate you, bless those who curse you, and pray for those who spitefully use you. To him who strikes you on the one cheek, offer the other also. And from him who takes away your cloak, do not withhold your tunic either. Give to everyone who asks of you. And from him who takes away your goods do not ask them back. And just as you want men to do to you, you also do to them likewise. But if you love

those who love you, what credit is that to you?
For even sinners love those who love them. And
if you do good to those who do good to you, what
credit is that to you? For even sinners do the
same. And if you lend to those from whom you
hope to receive back, what credit is that to you?
For even sinners lend to sinners to receive as
much back. But love your enemies, do good, and
lend, hoping for nothing in return; and your
reward will be great, and you will be sons of the
highest. For He is kind to the unthankful and
evil. Therefore be merciful, just as your Father
also is merciful. Judge not, and you shall not be
judged. Condemn not, and you shall not be
condemned. Forgive, and you will be forgiven.
Give, and it will be given to you: Good measure,
pressed down, shaken together, and turning
over will be put into your bosom. For with the
same measure that you use, it will be measured
back to you (Luke 6:27–38).

Did you read this carefully? Perhaps it would help if
you read the passage once more.

Kindness is loving your enemies, and we do that by
doing good. The passage refers to lending money and not

expecting anything in return. Kindness is being merciful. When we give to others in this way, God promises that much will be given to us.

- **It seeks to relieve the burden of others.** One of the fascinating usages of the word "kind" is found where Jesus said:

Come to Me, all you who labor and are heavy laden, and I will give you rest. Take My yoke upon You and learn from Me, for I am gentle and lowly in heart, and you will find rest for your souls. For My yoke is easy and my burden is light (Matthew 11:28-30).

The word "easy" is the Greek word translated "kind". The illustration pictures a yoke of oxen. A farmer, in ancient times, would train a new, inexperienced ox by having it walk alongside an experienced ox while not carrying the load. On the side of the yoke where the inexperienced ox was placed, the straps or ropes were loose. The inexperienced ox did not carry the load, but was simply learning how to plow by walking alongside the experienced ox.

Jesus Christ is carrying the load; He referred to "My

yoke". We learn by walking at His side, trusting Him to carry our burdens. He said that His burden is light; that's because He is carrying the load!

Kindness does not lay heavy burdens on others, but rather seeks to relieve the burdens that others are carrying. God's love is shown when a fellow believer does what he or she can to relieve you of the load you are carrying. Kindness was shown to me when a young man rushed to my aid as I was unloading boxes of books out of the trunk of my car. He did it with great joy and made me believe that it was an honor for him to do so.

Kindness was also shown to me when a friend saw the stress I was under, having a deadline to meet, and offered to help me by using his computer to print needed items for me. He had other work to do and what I was doing was not in his job description, but he truly wanted to help. He loves me, and it shows.

In review, what is kindness?

- It shows compassion for the needs of others.
- It desires to forgive.
- It does good to those who are enemies, and to those who are not thankful but evil.
- It seeks to relieve the burdens of others.

Part Five

The Negatives of Love

What Love Does Not Do

Chapter Five

The Negatives of Love

Love Does Not Envy

The word "love" does not appear in the Greek text in front of the words "does not envy" or in any of the eight negatives describing love. It appears only in front of the two beginning statements of I Corinthians 13:4, "The love suffers long" and, "The love is kind."

The word "envy" comes from a Greek word which, when transliterated into English, becomes our word "zealous". It appears in its various forms 34 times in the New Testament. It can mean "envy", "jealousy" or "indignation". The root word means "to seethe" or "to boil". It refers to emotions that are easily stirred up in all of us. God's love suffers long, or takes a long time to boil; it does not fly off the handle or react quickly with bitterness and anger.

In its good sense the word means "zealous" or "enthusiastic" but in its bad sense it means jealousy and carries with it the idea of bitterness and resentment, harboring attitudes that show competition to others. The text does not allow us to be jealous *sometimes*, it says that God's love is not jealous at all – case closed!

Joseph's brothers were jealous of him. They hated him because their father loved Joseph more than he loved them:

Now Israel loved Joseph more than all his children, because he was the son of his old age. Also he made him a tunic of many colors. But when his brothers saw that their father loved him more than all his brothers, they hated him and could not speak peaceably to him. Now Joseph dreamed a dream, and he told his brothers; and they hated him even more. So he said to them, "Please hear this dream which I have dreamed: There we were, binding sheaves in the field. Then behold, my sheaf arose and also stood upright; and indeed your sheaves stood all around and bowed down to my sheaf." And his brothers said to him, "Shall you indeed reign over us? Or shall you indeed have dominion over us?" So they hated him even more for his dreams and for his words. Then he dreamed still another dream and told it to his brothers, and said, "Look, I have dreamed another dream. And this time, the sun, the moon, and the eleven stars bowed down to me." So he told it to his father and his brothers; and his father rebuked him and said to him, "What is this dream that you have dreamed? Shall your mother and I and your brothers indeed come to bow down to the earth before you?" And his brothers envied him, but his father kept the matter in mind (Genesis 37:3-11).

Verse 4 says that the brothers hated him and could not speak peaceably to him. Verse 8 says that *"...they hated him even more"* for his dreams and his words to them. Verse 11 captures the root issue when it says that "his brothers envied him". Jealousy, envy, hatred – all these are contrary to God's love. Acts 7:9 confirms this issue when it says, *"The patriarchs, becoming envious, sold Joseph into Egypt."* The Greek word for "envious" is the same as in I Corinthians 13:4 when it tells us that love *"does not envy".*

When you are jealous over the attention or love shown to others rather than to you, this can lead to intense hatred for the person with whom you compare yourself. Jealousy is the desire to have the same thing for yourself that someone else has. There is another Greek word *(phthonos)* that refers to the desire to deprive another person of what he or she has. It is also translated "envy". Jealousy is a serious problem and can quickly destroy your joy and growth in the Lord.

One of our children needed some shelves in his room, and was very happy when he got them, but when our other son saw them, he said, "What about me? I need some shelves in my room, too!" My first thought was, "You should be glad to have your own room!" I soon realized that we were observing jealousy over what someone else has that we don't have. It's natural to act that way, but, it's not the way God's love responds. Our child was concluding that the fact that he did not receive shelves for his room as his brother did, indicated that his parents did not love him as much as they love his brother. That's the "Joseph problem" all over again! I reassured him of our love, and also made plans about his need for shelves!

Jealousy in the lives of adults can be even more damaging than the simple problems that children encounter in growing up. Jealousy is serious whenever it occurs and should be dealt with immediately, but adults have a tendency to harbor hatred and resentment much longer than children do.

In Acts 5:17, we observe the high priest, along with a group of Sadducees, who were angry over the miracles that were being performed by the apostles. The Bible says, *"They were filled with indignation [envy],"*

In Acts 13:45, the Jews of the synagogue in Antioch of Pisidia (central Turkey) saw the impact Paul and Barnabas had on multitudes who responded to their teaching and preaching. The passage says that when they saw the multitudes, *"They were filled with envy."* They began to contradict, blaspheme and oppose the things which the apostle Paul was teaching. Envy can cause us to lose perspective. We begin to justify our anger and opposition to others, and it becomes difficult for us to admit that the root problem is envy or jealousy.

In Romans 13:13, the apostle Paul uses the word "envy" in connection with drunkenness and sexual promiscuity. In rebuke of the Christians at Corinth (I Corinthians 3:3), he spoke of it as a manifestation of carnality and said, *"For where there are envy, strife, and divisions among you, are you not carnal and behaving like mere men?"* Galatians 5:20 lists "jealousies" as a part of the *"works of the flesh"*. James 3:14 speaks of "bitter envy" and says that its source is not the wisdom of God, but that which is *"earthly, sensual, demonic"* (James 3:15). Verse 16 adds, *"For where envy and self-seeking exist, confusion and every evil thing will be there.*"

God's love does not compare one person to another. It does not envy nor feel jealous of the successes, abilities, appearance or blessings of others. It does not feel hurt because another person is happy or honored. It rejoices with them and hurts with them when they hurt. God's love seeks the best for others and is not disappointed because another person's blessing does not belong to the person doing the loving.

John could hardly stand being in the presence of Tom. Tom was successful in business and well-liked by others. Tom seemed to have very few difficulties in his life and was always chosen before John. John noticed that the honors always went to Tom, and that people proclaimed his virtues and usually ignored the efforts which John had put forth, while frequently expressing appreciation for Tom's work.

Supposedly Tom and John were close friends, but both of them felt tension when they were together. John wanted more approval and resented Tom greatly. The whole situation became unbearable. One day John spoke angrily to Tom and lost control. All his bitterness poured out as he expressed his true feelings about Tom. Tom was shocked and unaware of John's feelings, even though he could feel the strain in their relationship at times.

After the outburst of anger by John, they both started to talk to each other in a deeper and more loving way. They discussed the problem openly, and assured each other of their support and prayers. John realized that his problem was rooted in envy and jealousy. Tom became more sensitive to John's feelings, and their overall relationship began to improve. Both knew that they needed God's love toward each other in spite of their differences and frequent disagreements. God's love is what we need!

Love Does Not Parade Itself

Everybody loves a parade! Yet, when an individual is "parading" himself in front of others in order to impress them or to receive attention and strokes, God's love is missing.

This is the only place in the Bible where this word is used. The Greek word from which this verb is taken refers to a braggart - somebody who reads his own press clippings and makes sure that everyone else knows about them!

An early church leader by the name of Clement of Alexandria says that this word means "to ornament oneself with the emphasis on the extraneous and useless". In other words, God's love does not boast about that which is unimportant and useless.

We often put the emphasis upon things that do not last and are not eternal. We boast about cars, clothes, trophies, awards, houses, boats, sports, etc. Jesus referred to this problem:

Do not lay up for yourselves treasures on earth, where moth and rust destroy and where thieves break in and steal; but lay up for yourselves treasures in heaven, where neither moth nor rust destroys and where thieves do not break in and steal. For where your treasure is, there your heart will be also (Matthew 6:19-21).

The world is "passing away", says I John 2:17. We are told not to love it. We brought nothing into this world and it is certain that we will take nothing out of it (I Timothy 6:7). Those who refuse to brag are those who understand that everything we have comes from God. We are to be stewards of what He has given us. I Corinthians 4:7 asks the question, *"What do you have that you did not receive?"*

I was in a friend's home admiring some trophies that he had won in various athletic contests. He seemed proud of them and they were displayed in a place where everyone who walked into his house would automatically notice them.

I asked him about their value. He laughed, and pointed to one of them that was already broken and was obviously a very cheap trophy. Those trophies were of no use to him and, with the passing of time, they held little value in his life. He said that they reminded him of what is **not** important, and he was getting ready to throw them all away. They were useless, and what was the point in bragging about them? We both agreed!

The sad thing about someone who brags over his achievements and accomplishments is that it has a tendency to drive others away rather than bring them closer. No one likes to be a friend of a braggart; it is irritating to listen to someone brag about unimportant things since it reveals a lack of love for people.

When you love with God's love, you learn to "boast in the Lord" rather than in yourself. Psalm 34:2 says, "*My soul shall make its boast in the Lord.*" Psalm 44:8 adds, "*In God we boast all day long.*" I Corinthians 1:31 quotes a passage in Jeremiah 9:24 when it says, *"He who glories, let him glory in the Lord."* A loving person learns to brag about Who God is and what God can do, rather than about what he or she can do.

Boasting can become such a part of you that you don't even notice when you are doing it. One example that affects me deals with the diplomas and degrees that I have achieved and have subsequently framed on beautiful plaques.

For quite a long time I had them hanging in my church office where everyone could see them, but one day it struck me: What was the purpose of those plaques hanging in my office? Was it to impress people? Was I using them to try to make people respect me or respond to me? That did it! I removed the plaques. I felt 100 percent better about myself and my ministry by that simple act. It was a little thing, but it was affecting me.

You don't have to impress people with plaques, trophies, awards, degrees, etc. Everything we are and have comes from the Lord. To Him be all the glory! I want to minister to people with a heart that boasts in the Lord, not in myself. And, frankly, that's not easy to do!

Love Is Not Puffed Up

Eight times in the New Testament, the Greek word for arrogance is used. In I Corinthians 13:4, the verb is in the middle voice in Greek which means that God's love does not puff itself up. The only one who can make you arrogant is yourself!

Arrogance refers to the inflation of one's importance, abilities, appearance or achievements. It seems closely related to our previous characteristic of God's love, "Does not brag". Proverbs 27:2 says, *"Let another man praise you, and not your own mouth; a stranger, and not your own lips."*

An example of arrogance is found in this illustration by Jesus:

Two men went up to the temple to pray, one a Pharisee and the other a tax collector. The Pharisee stood and prayed thus with himself, "God, I thank You that I am not like other men – extortioners, unjust, adulterers, or even as this tax collector. I fast twice a week; I give tithes of all that I possess." And the tax collector, standing afar off, would not so much as raise his eyes to heaven, but beat his breast, saying, "God be merciful to me a sinner!" I tell you, this man went down to his house justified rather than the other; for everyone who exalts himself will be abased, and he who humbles himself will be exalted (Luke 18:10-14).

Arrogance manifests a superior attitude. It thinks better of itself than it ought to think. It has an inflated opinion of itself, and does not face reality. It is the attitude of a person who loses sight of the grace and sovereignty of God. When a person begins to think that his or her talents are self-produced, that person is arrogant. God gives us all our talents and opportunities; there is nothing we have that we did not receive from Him.

You stop loving others when you inflate your own importance. We often do that when we compare ourselves with others which reveals a very insecure person! Arrogance depends upon constant evaluation with others. Arrogance seeks out people who are not quite as gifted or talented, and uses them as standards for evaluation. Arrogance criticizes and tears down another person whose abilities are greater or whose position in life carries more impact or authority than our own. It is extremely difficult for an arrogant person to show love to others.

I realized the importance of this when I received a letter from one of the people who attends our church. This person heard me say as I was preaching, "Do you understand what I'm saying?" I didn't think too much about it, but this person felt it was an arrogant remark. It suggested that I knew more than the people did and that it was difficult for them to understand what I was saying. After careful evaluation of this person's criticism, I realized that my remark could be interpreted that way. I did not want to reflect that kind of attitude. I did a little heart-searching in an effort to root out any arrogance that I might have felt.

I Corinthians 4:6 says, "...*that none of you may be puffed up on behalf of one against the other.*" Emphasizing the differences in people sometimes leads to the problem of arrogance. We are created by God and we are all different. The standard of measurement is not another person but what God Himself expects of us.

In I Corinthians 4:18, Paul referred to the fact that *"some are puffed up"* in their attitudes. He remarked,

But I will come to you shortly, if the Lord wills, and I will know, not the word of those who are puffed up, but the power (I Corinthians 4:19).

*You are puffed up, and have not rather
mourned, that he who has done this deed might
be taken away from among you* (I Corinthians
5:2).

Paul was referring to their toleration of sexual
immorality within the membership of the church. Their
arrogance made them reluctant to do what God's holy and
righteous standards would demand. They didn't want
anyone telling them what to do. But God's love does not
compromise with sin, though it is always tender toward
those who are struggling with sinful habits and practices. It
always seeks to help, not hurt or hinder.

In I Corinthians 8:1, we see the simple principle,
"Knowledge puffs up, but love edifies." In Colossians 2:18,
Paul spoke of the one who takes *"...delight in false humility
and worship of angels, intruding into those things which
he has not seen, vainly puffed up by his fleshly mind."*

We puff ourselves up when we think we know
everything, and are not willing to admit that we have much
to learn. We are also puffed up when we know what to do
but are insensitive to others around us who do not know
what we know.

While blowing up a balloon for my children one day, I thought about the words "puffed up". First, it took a good bit of effort on my part to blow up a particular balloon. Arrogance is like that – it's an effort and involves a lot of it! As I gazed at the balloon for a minute and thought about arrogance and being puffed up or inflated, I let go of the balloon and watched it sail around the room as its air was released.

As the balloon collapsed to the floor, I thought about how arrogance is like that balloon. All puffed up, it sails around boasting of its greatness, but then the truth is seen as the balloon collapses in a heap on the floor. A silly illustration? Maybe, but it made an impact on me that day. The balloon was attractive to my children as long as it was filled with air, but without the air, the fascination was gone. Our lives are often like that balloon. Our arrogance is simply a lot of air, nothing more ... nothing really significant or substantial. And after the air is released, well . . . enough said.

The Bible says:

Humble yourself in the sight of the Lord, and He will lift you up (James 4:1).

Love Does Not Behave Rudely

The root word for "rudely" is our English word "scheme" or "schematic". It refers to the shape of something. The King James Version says, *"Doth not behave itself unseemly."* The word deals with etiquette. We would translate literally, "is not without shape".

The word refers to outward appearance. It is important **how** something is said as well as **what** is said. Rudeness and bluntness are not the way of God's love. Love says the proper thing at the proper time in a loving way. Many of us mean well but are not sufficiently concerned with how our words affect others.

I was greeting people after a church service when a young man crowded into the line and forced his presence upon me, insisting that what he had to say was more important than the others. He was rude and blunt. He was acting unbecomingly. His manner and words were without shape. But true love is not rude; it is concerned about others.

The verb translated "does not behave rudely" is used in I Corinthians 7:36, which says:

If any man thinks he is behaving improperly

toward his virgin, if she is past the flower of her
youth, and thus it must be, let him do what he
wishes, he does not sin; let them marry.

This remark follows a discussion about the benefits of
remaining single. This might lead some Christian fathers to
believe that they would be doing the wrong thing if they
gave their daughters in marriage. Paul corrects that
possibility. The father was thinking that he would be acting
"improperly" or "unbecomingly" or "without shape" toward
his daughter if he let her marry when being single was of
such great benefit to the Lord's work.

The word "shape" might be better rendered "plan". It was
the plan of God with which the father was concerned. He
did not want to be unloving toward his daughter, nor in his
response toward God and His will.

In I Corinthians 12:23, the verb, "does not behave
rudely", is used as a noun when it refers to the
"unpresentable" parts of the body of Christ. These believers
are rude and blunt, usually unloving in their responses and
deficient in tact and etiquette. The Bible urges believers to
bestow more honor upon these believers who seem less
honorable.

The word is also used in Romans 1:27 to refer to "what is shameful". It is speaking of indecent acts committed by men who got involved sexually with other men. Such acts of sexual immorality are "without shape" or "acting unbecomingly". God's love does not act that way. It does not violate God's plan or will.

In Revelation 16:15 our Lord Jesus Christ speaks:

Behold, I am coming as a thief. Blessed is he who watches, and keeps his garments, lest he walk naked and they see his shame.

The word "shame" is from the same word translated in I Corinthians 13:5 *"does not behave rudely".* To be naked reveals a lack of etiquette and proper morals.

From these usages of the word used to describe God's love, we can piece together the idea behind one who "*does not behave rudely".* The "scheme" of things is based on the plan and will of God. The person who loves with God's love is without "scheme" or "plan" of his own. There is plenty of "shape" to what he says and does - God's plan, God's will. God's love is concerned about the **way** words are communicated to others as surely as **what** is communicated.

Laughing at a time of sorrow, rebuking when there is a need for encouragement, shouting when talking with only one person – all these responses are "without shape". They are rude because they lack kindness and proper timing. But true love from God is much different than this.

Love Does Not Seek Its Own

Love does not keep a hidden agenda, a secret list of things to accomplish in every relationship with other people. Love does not build a kingdom to the honor of itself. Love reaches out to the needs of others, expresses a willingness to help and does so without any other motives.

This characteristic of God's love is essential in human communication and relationship. It is never the habit of God's love to be seeking things that pertain to oneself. Instead, it is always interested in the burdens and needs of others.

Let nothing be done through selfish ambition or conceit, but in lowliness of mind let each esteem others better than himself. Let each of you look out not only for his own interests, but also for the interests of others (Philippians 2:3,4).

That is true humility, and that is true unselfish love. Regarding others as more important and their interests before yours is the beauty and glory of God's love.

It's tragic when we see only what affects ourselves. Many of us live in a world that shuts others out. We talk about ourselves and show interest only in what affects us. But God's love is greatly interested in other people. It has to care about others – that's what it's like.

The words, "does not seek", are in the present tense in the Greek language, indicating a continuous pattern. The self-centered person is continually seeking things that affect and interest himself. The word "seek" is also translated "zealous". Our idea of enthusiasm is based on this word. A selfish person is often enthusiastic about his own projects and accomplishments, zealously pursuing those things in which self is honored, promoted or helped.

Other people are rarely involved in the interests pursued by the selfish person. What is of interest to others is of no real concern to the selfish person. The selfish person sees others as merely a means to an end. The selfish person uses people to promote his own interests and work.

A father comes home from work tired, faces his

children's desires for his time and presence, and is immediately confronted with the need for God's love (and strength!). Shall he lie down for a few minutes and rest or get up and play with his children? Will he be selfish or loving? Reading a paper or playing a game may demonstrate a father's love ... or lack of it!

Selfishness is often communicated at a young age when a child is not taught to share, but rather builds his life around the word "mine". Children who grow up receiving everything they could ever want or desire often have problems with self-centeredness later in life.

Star or Team Player?

In athletics, one makes the choice of being the "star" or a "team player". The "star" (who has athletic ability) is endured, accepted and praised – until after the game. In the game of life, the "star" is not loving but selfish, but the "star" who uses others to get what he wants (popularity and fame) will soon discover that others will use him. In contrast, the "team player" develops concepts of sharing and ministering to others.

One of the great basketball players of all time is Michael Jordan of the Chicago Bulls. 1991 was his year – he won the NBA Player of the Year and the prize he had sought for several years - the NBA championship. In a crucial game in the series finals with the Los Angeles Lakers, commentators were asking whether Michael Jordan, as great as he is, could involve his entire team in the game and become unselfish, preferring to pass the ball to others rather than shoot the ball himself.

One of the great basketball games (for true fans!) of all time was the game in which Michael dazzled us all with his deft passing and his setting up of other team members for easy baskets because most of the Lakers were concentrating on him. What an example he was that night as he, the star, became the ultimate "team player"! It was a turning point for the Bulls ... now they were unstoppable. They played as a team and won the championship.

Marriage and Unselfish Love

When marital partners build their responses to each other on self-gratification, the seeds of decay have already been planted in their marriage. No one likes to be used. No one cares to be around the self-centered person. Selfishness drives people away; it's not attractive, and it can never minister to one's real needs.

The husband who will not go shopping with his wife because he doesn't like to shop (when she loves it) is a selfish person. The wife who will not go with her husband to the ball game that he enjoys attending (but she hates) is also unloving and selfish.

Marriage is a test of our love. While most married people would argue that their relationship is built on love, the habits and practices of many couples reveal the opposite. They rarely do things together and, frankly, many couples do not enjoy being together at all. They say things like, "I love her ... I just don't like her!" or, "I really love him... but I don't enjoy the things he likes to do!"

God's love is willing to sacrifice personal desires and plans for the benefit of the one loved. We are willing to do what others want to do even when it is not particularly enjoyable for us personally.

The phrase, "do your own thing", has affected all of us in today's culture, dominated as it is by the demand for individual rights. But this philosophy is rooted in selfishness. We feel we have a right to do whatever we please, regardless of how it affects others. Our liberties become license to sin and hurt others. But God's true love cares about the other person. It draws a line when the other person is left out; it considers the other person's view and listens carefully; it tries hard to understand and to get excited over helping someone else.

Examples of Unselfish Love

Matthew 20:28 says of our Lord Jesus Christ:

The Son of Man did not come to be served, but
to serve, and to give His life a ransom for many.

God's love was evident in Jesus Christ. He came for others, not Himself. Romans 15:2,3 points this out clearly when it exhorts us:

Let each of us please his neighbors for his good,
leading to edification. For even Christ did not
please Himself; but as it is written, "The
reproaches of those who reproached You fell on
Me."

Abraham demonstrated this unselfish love of God when he said to his nephew, Lot:

Is not the whole land before you? Please separate
from me. If you take the left, then I will go to the

*right; or, if you go to the right, then I will go to
the left* (Genesis 13:9).

Lot chose the well-watered plain of Jordan and wound
up as a permanent resident in the city of Sodom, known for
its sexual deviation and moral corruption. The selfish
person would have said, "As your uncle, I have a right to
choose first. You can have what's left!"

King David revealed an unselfish heart when he said:

*The Lord forbid that I should do this thing to my
master, the Lord's anointed, to stretch out my
hand against him, seeing he is the anointed of
the Lord* (I Samuel 24:6).

Saul tried many times to kill him. No one would have
complained or criticized David if he had taken advantage
of Saul on this occasion and killed him. But he did not act
selfishly. Instead, he waited on the plan and timing of God.
He demonstrated concern for King Saul in spite of what
Saul had done to him.

Are you selfish? God's love cannot seek the things that
promote oneself. His love forces you to be concerned and
deeply interested in the needs of other people.

Love Is Not Provoked

The King James Version of the Bible reads, *"...is not easily provoked".* It is somewhat of a mystery to me why the translators added the word "easily". It does not appear in the Greek text, and it weakens the point. God's love is **never** provoked! Not at all!

The Greek word translated "provoked" is from two root words: "alongside of " and "to sharpen". God's love is not "made sharp" by others. It does not get bitter by the reactions or attacks of other people.

The verb is also in the middle voice in Greek, meaning that it does not let itself get continually provoked. In other words, if you get provoked, it's **your** problem! You did it to yourself! It's easy to blame others or the circumstances around you.

Several years ago, I received a letter from a lady who was provoked and hurt over the reactions of others to her ministry. But she was not helping herself. She was overly sensitive to what others say. She often evaluated meaningless incidents as personal attacks upon her character and ministry. What is the answer for her? A giant dose of God's love! Her problem was a lack of God's love in her life, the very thing that she accused others of not having toward her.

Should We Ever Get Provoked?

It is right to get provoked at things and situations that are clearly wrong. In Acts 17:16, we learn that Paul was provoked over the idolatry in the city of Athens. If you want to get angry at something, then get provoked over idolatry.

While Paul waited for them at Athens, his spirit was provoked within him when he saw that the city was given over to idols.

It makes God angry as well. It is right to get provoked at sin and rebellion against God. However, it is not right to get provoked at people. Paul experienced that once in his relationship with Barnabas. We read about their division:

After some days Paul said to Barnabas, "Let us now go back and visit our brethren in every city where we have preached the word of the Lord, and see how they are doing." Now Barnabas was determined to take with them John called Mark. But Paul insisted that they should not take with them the one who had departed from them in Pamphylia, and had not gone with them to the work. Then the contention became so sharp that they parted from one another. And so Barnabas took Mark and sailed to Cyprus; but Paul chose Silas and departed, being commended by the brethren to the grace of God. And he went through Syria and Cilicia strengthening the churches (Acts 15:36-41).

This was a disagreement over John Mark going with them on their next missionary journey. Paul did not want to take him along because he was a "dropout" from a previous missionary trip (cf. Acts 13:13). Barnabas ("Son of Encouragement") had a heart for him, as well as being a relative. Paul and Barnabas got provoked at each other, and it caused them to separate from each other.

Regardless of your view as to whose fault it was, the real problem was a lack of God's love. God's love is never provoked at people, although it is often provoked at situations and practices that are wrong and sinful.

The Example of Jesus Christ

Consider the example of Jesus Christ:

Servants, be submissive to your masters with all fear, not only to the good and gentle, but also to the harsh. For this is commendable, if because of conscience toward God one endures grief, suffering wrongfully. For what credit is it if, when you are beaten for your faults, you take it patiently? But when you do good and suffer for it, if you take it patiently, this is commendable before God. For to this you were called, because Christ also suffered for us, leaving us an example, that you should follow His steps: "Who committed no sin, nor was guile found in His mouth"; who, when He was reviled, did not revile in return; when He suffered, He did not threaten, but committed Himself to Him Who judges righteously; Who Himself bore our sins in His own body on the tree, that we, having died to sin, might live for righteousness - by Whose stripes you were healed. For you were like sheep going astray, but have now returned to the Shepherd and Overseer of your souls (I Peter 2:18-25).

When He was reviled, He did not revile in return. This is the opposite side of "loving your enemies" (Matthew 5:43-48). It's easy to get upset with people to the point of wanting a "pound of flesh". You want to get even with them. Sometimes this leads to a permanent barrier between you and the person who provoked you. That bitterness can eat your heart out!

Never seek revenge! Leave that to God. Paul wrote:

Repay no one evil for evil. Have regard for good things in the sight of all men. If it is possible, as much as depends on you, live peaceably with all men. Beloved, do not avenge yourselves, but rather give place to wrath; for it is written, "Vengeance is mine, I will repay," says the Lord. "Therefore if your enemy hungers, feed him; if he thirsts, give him a drink; for in so doing you will heap coals of fire on his head." Do not be overcome by evil, but overcome evil with good (Romans 12:17–21).

Be upset with things that are wrong, but don't let that carry over to the people who are involved. Spiritual love, the love of God Himself, never gets provoked at people. After all, as we have learned, God's love is patient (longsuffering) and kind.

Love Thinks No Evil

The New American Standard Bible translates this phrase *"does not take into account a wrong suffered"*. The definite article in Greek is found in front of the word "evil". It refers to the particular evil which has made an attack on you. It is not referring to evil in general.

The great problem here is our ability to forgive. When we have been wronged, it is hard for us to forgive and forget. In modern Greek, the word "thinks" refers to an accountant. It means "to calculate". God's love does not spend time "calculating" the evil done in figuring how to "get even" or "get revenge". It refuses to dwell on it.

Philippians 4:8 gives a list of things to think about (same word – "to calculate") – things that are true, noble, just, pure, lovely, and of good report. These things are worthy of much thought. We are to let our minds dwell on these good things, not the wrong things done to us.

The longer you live, the more aware you become of how futile it is to get revenge. You hurt yourself deeply when you do not forgive. People are people, and there will be times when they will wrong you. You must learn to live with that and, most of all, learn to forgive.

When someone you love does something wrong to you, it especially hurts. It's easy to remember it, and to let the wrong stand as a barrier to a deeper and closer relationship. It's hard to forgive, and doubly hard to forget.

Many married couples have used a wrong of the past to hurt the other partner in the present. They are both hurt by this tactic and little good ever comes of it. How much sweeter it is to forgive, bury it and never bring it up again!

Several years ago, a married couple came to our house to talk about their anger and bitterness toward each other. It seems that the husband was involved ten years earlier in an affair that lasted almost two years. The wife became very bitter and unwilling to forgive. She made life miserable for him and, from a human perspective perhaps, he deserved it.

In her anger and her desire to hurt her husband, she had an affair also. She really didn't care about the man she was involved with and, in fact, hardly knew him. She just wanted to hurt her husband. The result was that it worked. His hurt turned to more bitterness and the shouting and accusations became a regular part of their home life. Their children, now teenagers, were greatly affected by all the anger and shouting.

In desperation, they both came to talk about their marital difficulties. The problem was a failure to forgive. The hurt can run so deep that we can't stop thinking about it. God's love *"thinks* [calculates] *no evil".* It no longer concentrates on it.

When you continue to rehearse and review another person's failures, and your mind constantly thinks about it and the hurt you have endured, you are lacking in God's love. Once a person has sought your forgiveness and confessed the sin or failure or wrong, it is now your responsibility to forgive and to stop calculating. Stop thinking about the hurt that was done to you and, above all, stop reminding the person who asked you for forgiveness about how much he or she damaged your heart and life. It is the lack of God's love that causes us to review, question, analyze and make the other person know how much we were hurt by what the person did to us, or what his or her actions caused.

A Christian friend found himself "calculating" against his wife because of something she had done. Before they were married, she had been unfaithful to him during the time of their engagement. But she had repented and sought forgiveness, and he had said to her at the time that he would forgive her. Now, 20 years later, he was using that incident to take revenge on something his wife had done. He hurt her deeply, as well as himself. As he said to me, "I don't know why I did that!" God's love was not controlling him at the time and when God's love is not operating, we are all susceptible to saying and doing terrible things that hurt others.

When you let your mind concentrate on the wrong done to you, you will find a great deal of bitterness and resentment toward the person who did the wrong to you. Don't continue to think about it! Unless you have God's love controlling you, your relationship with that person will be seriously damaged.

Romans 12:21 advises:

Do not be overcome by evil, but overcome evil with good.

That's the proper way to handle it – return good for evil. That's God's love in action! When people see that kind of reaction, they'll find it hard to believe! There can be only one explanation – the control of God's Holy Spirit in that person's life!

One of the commonest ways that married couples reflect this problem is by refusing to give the love and affection that the other partner needs and desires – all because that partner did or said something that offended the other partner. This often leads to more serious problems. It is better to forgive – always! Seeking revenge or trying to get even has proven to me to be one gigantic waste of time! Yet if I am not controlled by God's love, my old sinful nature automatically tries to get even when I am wronged.

A friend in the ministry wrote me a nasty letter one day. What he said about me was not true. He was very religious and spiritual in how he said it, and it still hurt very deeply. I immediately wrote a letter back, answering the accusations and defending myself. I cleverly began to accuse him of a failure to love. I said it so well, I was quite proud of myself.

Several weeks later the Lord convicted me of my attitude and my lack of love for that man. I quickly wrote him a letter, thanking him for what he had said and assuring him that the Lord had a purpose in it – that I had learned a great lesson through it. Then I expressed my love for him that, in spite of our disagreements, I deeply appreciated his ministry and his patience with me. It was such a joy to see how God used that letter to bind our hearts back together again. God's love really works!

The hardest thing to admit is that you are wrong. Maybe the wrong done to you is really wrong, but your attitude toward that wrong can also be wrong! How we need God's love and forgiveness! Think of what it would be like for all of us if God treated us with revenge for the ways in which we have wronged Him! Thanks be to God for His loving patience and continual forgiveness! We are so undeserving!

It helps me when I express kindness and loving words to someone who has wronged me. (That isn't my natural inclination!) The next time it happens to you, try to say something kind or loving to the person who has wronged you. First, ask God to help you to say it with love, not revenge. You'll be amazed at the results! I think we would all get along much better if we just stop "calculating" over what others do to us. God's love has no time for such calculation!

Second, seek ways to show kindness to the one who has wronged you. Perhaps a card or gift could be sent. Overcome the wrong by doing good. Pray for that person and ask God to show you how to treat him or her with love and good deeds.

Love Does Not Rejoice in Iniquity

I Corinthians 13:6 says, *"...does not rejoice in iniquity, but rejoices in the truth."* At the sight of evil and sin in others, God's love automatically refrains from rejoicing. God's love is saddened when hearing of the defeats and tragedies in believers' lives.

I'm reminded of a phone call years ago that told me of one of my believing friends who had fallen into moral sin. My heart was sad and heavy. There are some who would be glad if they knew about this. They would say that he got what he deserved, but that's not the way of God's love.

It's easy to be glad at another person's misfortune when it makes you look better. We sense a satisfaction within when our competition is defeated or even destroyed, but that's rooted in an unloving attitude. God's love rejoices in the truth, because the truth can set us free.

Gossip is frequently rooted in a lack of love for others. When we seem to take great pleasure in telling others about another person's faults, weaknesses or sins, we reveal a lack of God's love. God's love refuses to be happy when hearing of unrighteousness.

God's love resists a censorious spirit or a judgmental attitude. It knows of God's grace and forgiveness. It believes in healing and restoration. It speaks the good about others, not the evil.

I rejoiced greatly when brethren came and testified of the truth that is in you, just as you walk in the truth. I have no greater joy than to hear that my children walk in truth (III John 3,4).

One of the men in a former ministry of mine was known for his critical remarks of others. He often told others about people who had fallen into sin. He seemed to take pleasure in condemning them and saying things like, "They got what they deserved."

One day his wife shared with me his lack of love for her and their children. I should have known. God's love is different in its response toward the sins of others than what this man continually reflected in his life. No wonder his family did not sense his love for them! His unloving attitude toward others was evidence of his lack of God's love in his own heart and life.

I like what one lady said when hearing of a mutual

friend who had fallen into moral sin, "I can't believe that of him... as a matter of fact, I won't believe it until I hear it from his own lips!" I liked the way she defended our mutual friend. She took no delight in hearing of his sin, but instead was grieved over the very mention of that possibility!

> *Above all things have fervent love for one another, for love will cover a multitude of sins* (I Peter 4:8).

When God's love controls you, there is a commitment to the truth. So often people share things that others have told them without checking the accuracy of the information. They have no firsthand knowledge of the facts, but they feel at perfect liberty to pass along the information without verifying it. There is also the problem of how we share something. The truth is not always evident in the way people tell something. They may be telling the truth from their perspective, but it may not be the real truth. We need to be careful about accepting what others say without having substantial confirmation of the facts. God's love "rejoices with the truth". It wants the truth above anything else! It is not satisfied with mere hearsay. It does not tolerate gossip.

The word translated "evil" is the Greek word for

"unrighteousness". Righteousness is God's standard. When that is violated, love is not rejoicing. It is easy to be glad at another person's misfortune when it leads to your gain or puts you in a better light before others.

Love rejoices in the truth because there is always hope of redemption and repentance. Love does not give up easily. Love keeps quiet about the faults of others and seeks to build them up rather than tear them down. Love is very protective of others and is not happy when their faults, weaknesses or sins are exposed. How we need the love of God in all our relationships with others!

After stating the two positive characteristics of spiritual love, the love of God Himself, the apostle Paul lists eight facts of God's love in terms of what it will not or does not do. The eight negatives describe the two positives - longsuffering and kindness. If those two qualities are seen in our lives, then the following things will not be evident:

- Jealously or envy

- Boasting

- Arrogance

- Rudeness

- Selfishness

- Provoking; refusing to yield

- Calculating revenge; unforgiving attitude

- Rejoicing over the sins of others.

These eight negatives reveal to us what God's love refuses to do. They are natural tendencies within all of us. Without God's love controlling our lives, these eight negatives will become our normal responses in all we do and say. They remind us of our constant need of the Holy Spirit's power and control!

Part Six

The Attitudes of Love

How Love Reacts to Changing Circumstances

Chapter Six

The Attitudes of Love

Love Bears All Things

God's love primarily focuses on people. It is longsuffering and kind and it is not characterized by envy, bragging, arrogance, rudeness, selfishness, vindictiveness, pride, criticism or an unforgiving spirit. It is concerned about the needs, feelings and concerns of others.

But one of the fascinating aspects of spiritual love, the love of God Himself, is how it reacts to circumstances. While we don't love "things", love affects how we respond and react to various situations that occur in our lives. Things do not always turn out the way we planned or expected – in case you hadn't noticed! Changing circumstances are sometimes the barometer of our spiritual maturity. How do we react when things do not go the way we wanted?

- All Things

The first thing we must do is to establish the fact that all

things are a part of God's plan and will. Not everyone agrees with
that principle. In order to adjust to the things we do not
understand or appreciate, we resort to the opinion that God
allows these things but that He certainly wouldn't **cause** them!

Consider carefully what the Bible teaches:

*We know that all things work together for good to
those who love God, to those who are the called
according to His purpose* (Romans 8:28).

*Of Him and through Him and to Him are all things,
to whom be glory forever. Amen* (Romans 11:36).

God is the source ("of Him"), the channel ("through Him"),
and the object ("to Him") of everything! Nothing is left out; He
controls all things, is involved in all things and knows why all
things are happening as they are.

*In whom also we have obtained an inheritance,
being predestined according to the purpose of Him
who works all things according to the counsel of His
will* (Ephesians 1:11).

God is not a passive observer of the "all things" of life. He is
deeply involved in them, making sure that all that happens
accomplishes His will. There is a divine plan behind the chaos
and disorder of this world. Ecclesiastes 3:1 says, *To everything*

there is a season, a time for every purpose under heaven." Verse 11 teaches, *"He has made everything beautiful in its time."* In a great summary of God's sovereign control and purpose:

> *I know that whatever God does, it shall be forever.*
> *Nothing can be added to it, and nothing taken from*
> *it. God does it that men should fear before Him. That*
> *which is has already been, and what is to be has*
> *already been, and God requires an account of what*
> *is past* (Ecclesiastes 3:14,15).

The Bible places chance within the framework of God's control:

> *The lot is cast into the lap, but its every decision is*
> *from the Lord* (Proverbs 16:33).

We may "flip a coin," but God already knows how it will turn out. He even knows the fact that we would use that method to determine what to do.

The word "all" means everything or everyone, and yet sometimes it is controlled by what is in the context. "All men" may refer to a particular group or it may refer to the entire world. When we speak of "all things", we are referring to all the circumstances, events and situations in our lives.

Our understanding of God's sovereign control over all things deeply affects our attitudes and actions. Paul writes:

Be anxious for nothing, but in everything by prayer and supplication, with thanksgiving, let your requests be made known to God; and the peace of God, which surpasses all understanding, will guard your hearts and minds through Christ Jesus (Philippians 4:6,7).

We are not to worry about anything. No circumstance or situation in life is outside the realm of God's help. Therefore prayer should be our first response, not our last resort!

I can do all things through Christ Who strengthens me (Philippians 4:13).

My God shall supply all your need according to His riches in glory by Christ Jesus (Philippians 4:19).

Our confidence in the God of "all things" keeps us from undue worry and anxiety and leads us to trust Him in every situation of life, knowing that He will give us the grace and strength to handle each matter and supply our need for it. Our response should be what Paul wrote:

In everything give thanks; for this is the will of God in Christ Jesus for you (I Thessalonians 5:18).

If God is controlling everything (and He is!), then we should express thanks for His control and purpose. Though we may not understand why things have happened as they have, He does and we can rely upon His sovereign purpose as He works all things for our good and His glory.

Love Bears All Things

The word for "bears" does not refer to endurance, but rather to protection. It is used seven times in the New Testament – four as a verb and three as a noun. The noun refers to the roof of a house (Matthew 8:8, Mark 2:3, Luke 7:6). In modern Greek, the word means the same as in the *koine* (common) Greek of the New Testament.

It is the idea that God's love protects or covers; it offers shelter:

Above all things have fervent love for one another,
for love will cover a multitude of sins (I Peter 4:8).

We need to forgive the wrongs that people do to us, but we also need to protect and cover what was done. God's love reacts to difficult circumstances with protection. This is not hiding from the truth or sweeping it under a rug. Love does not broadcast failures, sins and weaknesses of others to those who are not involved directly in the incident or situation involving those matters.

Sometimes the "all things" we are to cover and protect are seen as threats to our own security. It is difficult under those circumstances to cover and protect. When your friend is exposed for some reason as being weak and sinful, what is your first reaction? To cover and protect? Or is it to display publicly (share with a few "close" friends!) and let others know how bad he or she is? A loving friend is one to whom you can trust your character and reputation when you are out of town. There is no fear or insecurity when God's love is present.

- David and Jonathan

One of the most beautiful and inspiring stories of loving friendship is that of David and Jonathan. In spite of efforts by homosexuals to prove that their relationship was a sexual one, there is absolutely no evidence of that and, in fact, it would be difficult to accept the statements of the Bible about King David and his integrity and loyalty to God if that were the case. David's relationship with Jonathan was deep, personal and intimate, but did not involve sexual activity between them.

I Samuel 18:1 says, *"The soul of Jonathan was knit to the soul of David, and Jonathan loved him as his own soul."* The story of Jonathan's protective love is seen when his father, King Saul, was plotting to kill his friend, David. The Bible provides the background:

Saul spoke to Jonathan his son and to all his servants, that

they should kill David; but Jonathan, Saul's son,
delighted much in David. So Jonathan told David,
saying, "My father Saul seeks to kill you. Therefore
please be on your guard until morning, and stay in a
secret place and hide. And I will go out and stand
beside my father in the field where you are, and I will
speak with my father about you. Then what I
observe, I will tell you." Now Jonathan spoke well of
David to Saul his father, and said to him, "Let not the
king sin against his servant, against David, because
he has not sinned against you, and because his works
have been very good toward you. For he took his life
in his hands and killed the Philistine, and the Lord
brought about a great salvation for all Israel. You
saw it and rejoiced. Why then will you sin against
innocent blood, to kill David without a cause?" So
Saul heeded the voice of Jonathan, and Saul swore,
"As the Lord lives, he shall not be killed." Then
Jonathan called David, and Jonathan told him all
these things. So Jonathan brought David to Saul, and
he was in his presence as in times past (I Samuel
19:1-7).

What wonderful love Jonathan had for David! David
returned the favor to Jonathan after his death:

David said, "Is there still anyone who is left of
the house of Saul, that I may show him kindness

for Jonathan's sake?" And there was a servant of the house of Saul whose name was Ziba. So when they had called him to David, the king said to him, "Are you Ziba?" And he said, "At your service!" Then the king said, "Is there not still someone of the house of Saul to whom I may show the kindness of God?" And Ziba said to the King, "There is still a son of Jonathan who is lame in his feet." So the king said to him, "Where is he?" And Ziba said to the king, "Indeed he is in the house of Machir the son of Ammiel, in Lo Debar." Then King David sent and brought him out of the house of Machir the son of Ammiel, from Lo Debar. Now when Mephibosheth the son of Jonathan, the son of Saul, had come to David, he fell on his face and prostrated himself. Then David said, "Mephibosheth?" and he answered, "Here is your servant!" So David said to him, "Do not fear, for I will surely show you kindness for Jonathan your father's sake, and will restore to you all the land of Saul your grandfather; and you shall eat bread at my table continually" (II Samuel 9:1-7).

David took care of Mephibosheth, the son of Jonathan, for the rest of his life because of his great love for Jonathan. It was Jonathan who showed (by what he did for David in front of his father, King Saul) that he had the kind of love that "bears" or covers all things.

God's love protects and covers those we love. It is not love when you inform others of how your friends have failed or sinned against God. It is not love when you do not prevent your friend from falling into danger, disaster or embarrassment. It is not love when you do not defend your friend's character or reputation in his absence.

The love that bears or covers all things is the love that puts up with minor points of irritation in others. It tolerates inconvenience and weakness, with kindness and protectiveness. It seeks to exalt the virtues of another, not the vices. It presents positive hope, not negative disappointment and defeat.

Mary needed the job, and her friend Alice knew it. Mary struggled with previous jobs and her skill levels were not what some of her jobs demanded, but she was faithful and a hard worker. When Alice was asked by her company about Mary, who had applied for a job, Alice knew that she had the influence to either recommend her or discourage her employer from hiring her. Alice, as a believer, did not want to lie, but the love of God caused her to protect Mary.

Alice told her employer that Mary was one of the most conscientious and hard-working people she had ever known and that, if given a job which matched her skill level, she would be a great employee and very productive. Her boss was impressed and hired Mary. Mary has done a great job and the areas where she has difficulty have never been exposed – thanks to Alice. Alice revealed that spiritual love was controlling her.

Love Believes All Things

Forms of the word, "believes", appear 559 times in the New Testament. The verb is used 248 times and is a fundamental word in Christian vocabulary. It involves trust. It is not merely intellectual assent, but describes dependence upon something or someone. The faith of the Bible implies an object to be trusted.

God's love reacts to the "all things" of life with trust and belief that God has a purpose and that, though we do not understand why things happen as they do, He does. When we say that love "believes all things", we are not talking about being naive or gullible. It does not mean that we no longer think about things or evaluate situations. It doesn't mean that we avoid getting facts about circumstances and events or that we simply believe whatever is told to us. That, of course, is ridiculous and can get you into a great deal of trouble in your life.

This phrase speaks of quiet confidence in everything that is happening. You know that it is for your good and God's glory. It is characterized by peace, not worry. Thanksgiving flows from the heart of one who "believes all things". There is a calm assurance that everything will be all right. When God's love is controlling, we can relax and be confident that our sovereign God is doing all things well.

- When Bad Things Happen

Much of life is not category "good" from our point of view. Bad things do happen. A child is drowned in a pool in the home of the parents, as happened once in our community. Can these parents believe all things? A young man without any evidence of criminal activity was shot to death by a gang driving by in a truck. They didn't know him and he had done nothing to provoke them. It was a senseless killing. Can we believe that all things have a purpose?

Job lived about 4,000 years ago and his story is an inspiration to people even today. The Bible says (Job 1:11) that he was *"blameless and upright, and one who feared God and shunned evil."* He had seven sons and three daughters, and God blessed this man with enormous wealth. The Bible says that, *"This man was the greatest of all the people of the East"* (Job 1:3).

The story of Job deals with why bad things happened to good people. Satan was involved, challenging God's protection and blessing of Job. Satan argued that Job would not follow the Lord if things went bad for him. So God allowed Satan to test Job, only permitting him to do what God would allow. As a result, Job lost his possessions and his family.

Job reflected on God's purposes and made this remarkable statement:

Naked I came from my mother's womb, and naked shall I return there. The Lord gave, and the Lord has

taken away; blessed be the name of the Lord (Job
1:21).

The Bible says that "*in all this Job did not sin nor charge God
with wrong*" (Job 1:22). Incredible!

Job's wife, however, did not see things that way. After
watching the tragedies and then observing the physical affliction
that came to Job as painful boils covered his body, his wife said:

*Do you still hold to your integrity? Curse God and
die!* (Job 2:9).

Job Responded:

*You speak as one of the foolish women speaks. Shall
we indeed accept good from God, and shall we not
accept adversity?* (v. 10).

The Bible adds, *"In all this Job did not sin with his
lips."*

Some of the most depressing conclusions ever put in print
are found in the book of Job as Job and his friends try to
understand the reasons of God behind the tragedies of life. Job
said of his friends' advice: *"Miserable comforters are you all!"* (Job
16:2).

God speaks directly with Job after he experiences the frustrations of his friends trying to give him reasons for the bad things that had happened. God basically tells Job that he has no right to question Him and certainly does not possess the power to do anything about the "things" of life that seem so bad. Job's response is a classic:

I know that You can do everything, and that no purpose of Yours can be withheld from You. You asked, "Who is this who hides counsel without knowledge?" Therefore I have uttered what I did not understand, things too wonderful for me, which I did not know. Listen, please, and let me speak; You said, "I will question you, and you shall answer Me." I have heard of You by the hearing of the ear, but now my eye sees You. Therefore I abhor myself, and repent in dust and ashes (Job 42:2-6).

Job confesses that he does not understand, but that he has full confidence in God Who does. He acknowledges that God is a purposeful God and that He has reasons behind all that happens in our lives. The Bible says (Job 42:12) that *"the Lord blessed the latter days of Job more than his beginning."*

When God's love is controlling us, there is a strong and calm assurance that the "all things" of life have a divine purpose and that nothing happens by chance or coincidence.

Bob and Susan could not understand why God would not give them a child. All the medical exams they participated in revealed no particular problem as to why Susan could not get pregnant. In the course of time, God laid the burden on their heart to adopt. They have adopted several children now and also have had children of their own. They speak powerfully now of the purposes of God in their struggles. God gave them a heart for children that they would never otherwise have had.

To hear Richard now is a miracle! When the auto accident several years ago destroyed his legs, he became bitter and resentful. His attitudes were hard to endure and people hated to be around him. God's love was missing but through the kindness of the Lord, another handicapped person brought him a clear perspective of God and His purposes. Today Richard is being used by God to touch the lives of many others as he speaks powerfully about God's sovereignty and purposeful actions.

Debbie was heartbroken. The young man she loved – the one she wanted to marry – broke up with her and later married her best friend! How could God do this to her? For months she was depressed and rebellious. She stopped going to church, resisted her parents and refused to listen to anyone's counsel. In desperation she started to take drugs and consumed a great deal of alcohol but the pain inside her was growing, not diminishing.

Through a Christian nurse who happened to run into Debbie at a rehabilitation center, Debbie started to listen. She wanted help and freedom from the pain she felt inside. Debbie confessed her bitterness and began to understand the love of God for her. She no longer drinks or takes drugs and, best of all (from her perspective), God brought a fine Christian young man into her life to love her.

Debbie has learned what thousands of others have: God's love believes all things, that everything in life has a divine purpose and that God is working all to His glory and our good.

When Bill took his life, it was not easy for me to accept God's plan and purpose. He was a friend and I enjoyed many good times with him. His suicide note was beautiful, but also tragic. Through his funeral service, which I conducted, several people came to know Jesus Christ as their Lord and Savior. I still don't understand everything that happened, but I know that God used it for His glory and so I continue to believe the "all things" of life, even those things I don't understand.

Sometimes we learn of God's purpose behind the tragedies of life and we are encouraged, or at least sustained by the knowledge that God's hand is governing all things. However, much of what happens, we do not understand. It is more difficult during those times to trust God's ways and reasons and not become bitter. Job did not understand, but he put his trust in the One Who does - our wonderful Lord!

Love Hopes All Things

Hope is a beautiful word, helping us to take another step. Used 54 times as a noun and 31 times as a verb, it is the heart and soul of the Christian message. We have hope because of the promises of God.

The phrase "hopes all things" is characteristic of an optimistic heart. It is the quality of someone who is continually looking to the future. It is based on what God can do. God's Word gives us hope based on the ability of God Himself:

> *To Him Who is able to do exceeding abundantly above all that we ask or think, according to the power that works in us, to Him be glory in the church by Christ Jesus throughout all ages, world without end. Amen* (Ephesians 3:20,21).

Nothing is too difficult for God, so the one who "hopes all things" sees the difference that a loving God can make.

God's love is not pessimistic but optimistic. It always hopes for the best. In a discussion one day with another Christian worker, we were evaluating a certain person's lifestyle. For many years this person had proven to be a certain kind of person and, though there were repeated efforts to give him another chance, he continually failed to live up to the expectations of others.

Another occasion had arisen which afforded this individual another chance. Human nature and factual evidence told us to give up on him, but love said otherwise. Fortunately, love overruled and he was given another chance.

To the amazement of all of us, he began to produce for the Lord and his whole lifestyle changed! Thanks to love, things are different now in his life. A good lesson for all of us! Love is willing to risk for the benefit of others. Sometimes you have to "take a chance" when human reason says otherwise. Love does not give up easily.

- Hope and God's Promises

One of the most important understandings about the way spiritual love operates is that it has confidence in what God can do because it relies upon the promises of God and not the performances of people.

In a wonderful discussion about God's salvation and hope, Romans 5:1-5 says:

Therefore, having been justified by faith, we have peace with God through our Lord Jesus Christ, through Whom also we have access by faith into this grace in which we stand, and rejoice in hope of the glory of God. And not only that, but we also glory in tribulation, knowing that tribulation produces perseverance; and perseverance, character; and

character, hope. Now hope does not disappoint,
because the love of God has been poured out in our
hearts by the Holy Spirit Who was given to us.

In Romans 8:18-25, we have a discussion about present
suffering and future hope. In verses 24 and 25 we read:

We were saved in this hope, but hope that is seen is
not hope; for why does one still hope for what he
sees? But if we hope for what we do not see, then we
eagerly wait for it with perseverance.

Love is patient because it understands the promises of God
and knows that our hope will one day be realized when those
promises are fulfilled. When a believer is dying of terminal
illness and the body is decaying rapidly, the hope of bodily
resurrection sustains us during the pain and suffering. The love
of God which is shed abroad in our hearts by the Holy Spirit of
God causes us to "hope all things". We have confidence because
of God's promises.

Jesus said:

Heaven and earth will pass away, but My words will
by no means pass away (Matthew 24:35).

Jesus said in John 14:3, *"I will come again"* and believers
everywhere are relying upon that promise! We thus have hope
and we have the kind of love available to us that will cause us to

"hope all things".

The love that "hopes all things" is also aware of God's plan for the future. Things are going to get better - it's just a question of when! When the Lord Jesus Christ comes back there are going to be some dramatic changes - praise God! The "all things" of life can look mighty discouraging at times except for the sovereignty of God. God is working "all things" for His glory and our good. We can relax and know that they will turn out for the best. We have nothing to fear in this regard. His love puts that fear out of our hearts and replaces it with a confidence, a solid hope, built on the character of God Himself.

Hebrews 6:13-20 speaks of God's promises and the stability which our hope gives to us:

When God made a promise to Abraham, because He could swear by no one greater, He swore by Himself, saying, "Surely blessing I will bless you, and multiplying I will multiply you." And so, after he had patiently endured, he obtained the promise. For men indeed swear by the greater, and an oath for confirmation is for them an end of all dispute. Thus God, determining to show more abundantly to the heirs of promise the immutability of His counsel, confirmed it by an oath, that by two immutable things, in which it is impossible for God to lie, we might have strong consolation who have fled for refuge to lay hold of the hope set before us. This hope

we have as an anchor of the soul, both sure and
steadfast, and which enters the Presence behind the
veil, where the forerunner has entered for us, even
Jesus, having become High Priest forever according
to the order of Melchizedek.

Our hope is an anchor of the soul that gives stability to our
hearts as we await the fulfillment of God's promises. God's Word
backs up His promises. His character is clear; He cannot lie. All
will come to pass.

• Abraham and Hope

A practical illustration of how God's love will give us a
confidence, a hope based on God's veracity and His wonderful
promises is found in the life of Abraham:

Who, contrary to hope, in hope believed, so that he
became the father of many nations, according to
what was spoken, "So shall your descendants be."
And not being weak in faith, he did not consider his
own body, already dead (since he was about a
hundred years old), and the deadness of Sarah's
womb. He did not waver at the promise of God
through unbelief, but was strengthened in faith,
giving glory to God, and being fully convinced that
what He had promised He was also able to perform
(Romans 4:18-21).

Abraham and Sarah were old. At 99 years, Abraham was impotent, unable to produce seed for children to be born. Sarah was 89 years old and barren. Yet God said that in one year, they would have a child. Sarah laughed at this promise and the Lord responded, "Is anything too hard for the Lord?" The boy who was born was named Isaac, which means "laughter" in Hebrew, a reminder that God is able to do great and mighty things and that our hope is in the Lord, not in the human obstacles that might keep us from believing in what God can do.

Psalm 38:15 says, *"In You, O Lord, I hope."* Psalm 39:7 adds, *"My hope is in You."* The psalmist cries out in Psalm 71:5, *"You are my hope, O Lord God; You are my trust from my youth."* Verse 14 adds, *"I will hope continually, and will praise You yet more and more."* Psalm 119:81 says, *"I hope in Your word."* Psalm 146:5 summarizes:

Happy is he who has the God of Jacob for his help,
whose hope is in the Lord his God.

Love takes a hopeless situation and believes the best about it. Love doesn't give up on anything or anyone. Love believes that because of Who God is, circumstances can change for the better. Love sees that the "bad things" of life can turn out for the better when God works out His marvelous plan and purpose through them.

Love Endures All Things

The Greek word translated "endures" is also translated by the word "patience". It is not the word of I Corinthians 13:4 where we read that God's love "suffers long". That is a word dealing with patience toward people. The word in verse 7 refers to patience toward things or circumstances. It is used 17 times in the New Testament.

The love that "endures all things" is the one that can stand the pressure when things are not going right. The Greek word means "to bear up under" or "to remain under". The word is never used of God. God is never said to be in need of patience toward things, since He already controls everything.

Even after all human hope is gone, God's love will patiently endure for Jesus' sake. I have seen this many times in the case of the terminally ill. When cancer afflicts the people of God and all human hope is gone for possible recovery, when the words of the doctor reveal a limited period of time in which to live on this earth, that's a great opportunity for God's love to take over! The love of God can endure when everything else can't.

James tells us about patience:

My brethren, count it all joy when you fall into various trials, knowing that the testing of your faith produces patience. But let patience have its perfect work, that you may be perfect and complete, lacking nothing (James 1:2-4).

The trials of life are used by God to produce patience or endurance. God's love sustaining us will help us to endure a difficult situation. God's love can sustain you in the deepest trial and in the darkest night. Deuteronomy 33:27 says, *"The eternal God is your refuge, and underneath are the everlasting arms."* What wonderful security during the trials and difficulties of life!

God's love endures the circumstances of every day that produce impatience in most of us. We are impatient with the speed and quality of the work that others do, but God's love endures. We are impatient at the little inconveniences of life, such as traffic on the freeway and long lines at stores or offices, but God's love changes the picture and allows us to relax. God's love concentrates on what is really important, and sees His gracious hand behind everything that is happening in our lives.

- When You Don't Deserve What Happened

Often bad things occur in our lives that we do not deserve. At that point, we need to rest in the love of God and know that He has a purpose in it all. I Peter 2:19, 20 mentions this problem:

This is commendable, if because of conscience toward God one endures grief, suffering wrongfully. For what credit is it if, when you are beaten for your faults, you take it patiently? But when you do good and suffer for it, if you take it patiently, this is commendable before God.

If we suffer for our own faults, it is not a big deal that we are able to endure the experience and its consequences. But if we suffer wrongfully, and then take it patiently, that is commendable before God. It is God's love that helps us to endure all things.

Jesus said:

Blessed are those who are persecuted for righteousness' sake, for theirs is the kingdom of heaven. Blessed are you when they revile and persecute you, and say all kinds of evil against you falsely for my sake. Rejoice and be exceedingly glad, for great is your reward in heaven, for so they persecuted the prophets who were before you (Matthew 5:10-12).

God's love endures even when it is mistreated and persecuted without a just cause.

• Our Reaction

Let's face it – "all things" aren't always to our liking. It is one thing to believe intellectually that God is in control, but quite another thing to relax emotionally in times of stress, when the "all things" are going a different direction than we had planned or hoped for.

Our reaction to circumstances is often a barometer of God's love. When His love controls, we relax more and depend more upon Him. We recognize that things are always changing and though we do not know how they will turn out, He does!

When you are handling "all things" correctly, there is a spirit of thankfulness and joy in your heart (Ephesians 5:20; I Thessalonians 5:18). There is a certain peace governing your emotional response to things that happen. People like being around you in times of pressure. You make them feel at ease and worthwhile.

You seem to see the importance of what is happening for all concerned when you are controlled by God's love. You don't unleash your impatience at people. You're easy on them and loving to them. You're very protective and always defending the motives of those you love. Their character and reputation is in good hands when left with you.

We're wasting valuable time when we get upset over changing circumstances. There is a purpose behind them even when we are not aware of it (Ecclesiastes 3:1ff.). Have you ever had one of those days when nothing seemed to go right? That has happened to me. One day, I was absolutely confused as to why God would allow things to develop as they had that particular day.

But in the midst of that "mess" (from my perspective, of course!), God gave me an opportunity to minister to a needy heart that would otherwise never have occurred. During most of this time, I could not understand what was happening but when it was all over, I once again saw the loving hand of God behind it all!

May God give us all His perspective of what is happening. He is in control and His love can control us in "all things" of life.

Part Seven

The Greatness of Love

Why Love Excels All Other Pursuits in Life

Chapter Seven

The Greatness of Love

Love Never Fails

The last six verses of I Corinthians 13 are majestic and beautiful in describing the greatness of God's love. It is the *"more excellent way"* (I Corinthians 12:31), better than all the wonderful gifts which God the Holy Spirit has distributed among the believers.

Love never fails. But whether there are prophecies, they will fail; whether there are tongues, they will cease; whether there is knowledge, it will vanish away. For we know in part and prophesy in part. But when that which is perfect has come, then that which is in part will be done away. When I was a child, I spoke as a child, I understood as a child, I thought as a child; but when I became a man, I put away childish things. For now we see in a mirror, dimly, but then face to face. Now I know in part,

but then I shall know just as I also am known.
And now abide faith, hope, love, these three, but
the greatest of these is love (I Corinthians 13:8–
13).

Gifts, as wonderful as they are, will not last forever ...
but God's love will. The desire for spiritual gifts is proper (I
Corinthians 14:1) but not the highest pursuit of the
believer. Next to glorifying God (I Corinthians 10:31) and
reflecting it, is to love God and other people. Jesus spoke
these words about the greatness of love:

You shall love the Lord your God with all your
heart, with all your soul, and with all your mind.
This is the first and great commandment. And
the second is like it: You shall love your neighbor
as yourself. On these two commandments hang
all the Law and the Prophets (Matthew 22:37–
40).

God's love is the greatest! Loving God is the first and
greatest commandment, and loving other people is second
to it. Everything else pales into the background. The highest
pursuit is to glorify God by loving Him with all your heart,
mind, and soul – and then to pour that love into others.

The Inability of Certain Gifts to Last Forever

Spiritual gifts are greatly misunderstood and abused. They are wonderful blessings when God's love is controlling the person exercising the gift, but they can become curses when His love is absent. Love is more important than spiritual gifts but it takes a measure of maturity and growth to know why.

The key phrase in this section of Scripture is, "Love never fails." The Greek literally reads, "The love never at any point of time is failing." It never fails to be effective or to accomplish things. It never lacks force or power. It always works! Other good things (like spiritual gifts) can fail, both in time and under certain circumstances. But God's love never fails! We need it more than anything else in our life.

To illustrate the unfailing nature of love and its absolute importance to our lives and ministries, the apostle Paul reveals the temporary nature of certain gifts. He mentions three gifts, or the results of three gifts, in I Corinthians 13:8:

Whether there are prophecies, they will fail; whether there are tongues, they will cease; whether there is knowledge, it will vanish away.

The word "whether" *(elite)* can be translated, "if, at this point in time, and it is so". In other words, there is no doubt about the existence of these gifts. The word "whether" in the grammatical construction of the Greek language in this passage refers to that which is true. We might use the English word "since". We could translate this, "Since at this point in time there are prophecies ...." At the writing of I Corinthians (around 50-52 A.D.), the gifts of prophecy, tongues and knowledge were definitely in operation.

When commenting on prophecy and knowledge, the apostle Paul uses the same phrase in Greek, translated, "They will fail" and, "It will vanish away." The word "prophecies" refers to the content, not the proclamation. The result of the gift of prophecy is "prophecies". The word "knowledge" is, of course, in the singular as it always is.

The phrase, "...will fail" or "...will vanish away", suggests a phasing out over a period of time. It can be translated "to render inoperative" or "to become ineffective". At the writing of I Corinthians, they (prophecies and knowledge) were serving an important purpose, but something better was coming which would eliminate the need for them.

When Paul refers to "tongues" he changes the verb from "fail" or "vanish away" to "cease". Tongues will come to an abrupt stop. Prophecies and knowledge will be replaced by something better, but tongues will not be replaced. They will cease to be needed because of what is coming.

Prophecies and knowledge in this passage both refer to revelation from God. Tongues were needed as long as prophecies and knowledge were still being communicated. At the time of writing I Corinthians (one of the first epistles of Paul), the "revelation" of New Testament truth was incomplete. A portion of what the New Testament now contains had been put into writing by the time Paul wrote this letter to Corinth, but there was a great deal more to follow, much of which would be revealed by the Apostle Paul (as well as John, James, Jude and Peter). Tongues were necessary until the time when "prophecies" and "knowledge" would be phased out.

When Will Prophecies and Knowledge Be Phased Out?

If you read I Corinthians 13:8 carefully, you discover that the point in time at which "prophecies" and "knowledge" will be phased out is the same time at which "tongues" will cease to exist. Naturally, the great debate is over the point in time when this would occur.

If "tongues" are still in operation today, the "prophecies" and "knowledge" are still being communicated by God to men. That is a dangerous position! Can we add new revelation to what is contained in the 66 books of the Bible? Many cults and religious groups believe that this is, in fact, the case. That is why they have additional revelation which they treat with equal honor and respect as the Bible itself.

Why Tongues ?

The purpose of "tongues", according to I Corinthians 14:22, is that they are "...*for a sign, not to those who believe but to unbelievers*". In I Corinthians 14:21, we have a quotation from Isaiah 28:11,12. The people of Israel were not responding to God's revelation and God used "tongues" (the language of the Assyrians, who would bring God's judgment upon them) to confirm the authority and accuracy of His revelation to them through the prophets.

Jesus said in Mark 16:17-20 that tongues were a part of those signs that God would use to "confirm the word" (v. 20). The Book of Hebrews lays out the argument:

Therefore we must give the more earnest heed to the things we have heard, lest we drift away. For if the word spoken through angels proved steadfast, and every transgression and disobedience received a just reward, how shall we escape if we neglect so great a salvation, which at the first began to be spoken by the Lord, and was confirmed to us by those who heard Him, God also bearing witness both with signs and wonders, with various miracles, and gifts of the Holy Spirit, according to His own will? (Hebrews 2:1-4).

We cannot escape the judgment of God if we reject His Word. This passage tells us that God's Word was spoken first by the Lord, and then it was "confirmed" (same word as Mark 16:20) unto us by "...*those who heard Him, God also bearing witness both with signs and wonders, with various miracles, and gifts of the Holy Spirit.*" The word "those" refers to the apostles to whom God directly communicated New Testament truth. Their message was "confirmed" (a legal term meaning to authenticate as being genuine) by miraculous signs, gifts of the Spirit. II Corinthians 12:12 concurs with this when it says that "...*the signs of an apostle were accomplished among you with all perseverance, in signs and wonders and mighty deeds.*"

As long as God was giving new revelation through His apostles and prophets (cf. Ephesians 2:20; 3:5), "tongues" were needed to authenticate them and their message. These gifts, prophecies, knowledge and tongues were temporary. A point in time was coming in which they would no longer be needed. A point in time was coming when God's revelation would be finished... completed!

Why Are the Gifts Temporary?

Two reasons are given as to why these gifts will not be permanent:

- Because they give only partial understanding. I Corinthians 13:9 says, *"For we know in part and we prophesy in part."* Paul realized that he (in spite of the abundance of revelation given to him) did not have the complete truth; he had only partial understanding. As he wrote I Corinthians, it was not complete; there was more coming.

- Because something is coming that will bring complete understanding. I Corinthians 13:10 says, *"But when that which is perfect has come, then that which is part will be done away."* The words "has come" indicate a particular point in time. What is coming is described as "that which is perfect".

What Is "Perfect"?

This Greek word is used in its various forms about 75 times in the New Testament. In all these passages, we find about four major ideas in the meaning of the word "perfect":

- It is used of that which is whole or complete. It means nothing is left out. It refers to sacrifices that are without blemish. God's love is called "perfect" in I John 4:18. Perfect love doesn't lack for anything. In that passage, it does not have room for fear.

In Matthew 5:48, we are told to be "perfect" as our heavenly Father is. It is referring to the matter of loving our enemies. In order for us to be complete or total in our love, we must love our enemies as well as our friends.

- It is used for maturity. The Greek philosophers (like Plato and Aristotle) used it when referring to the end of the learning process. It meant that there was no need for further advancement. The Bible uses it in this way:

Him we preach, warning every man and teaching every man in all wisdom, that we may

present every man perfect in Christ Jesus
(Colossians 1:28).

- It is used for biological growth. Closely related
  to maturity, this usage refers to that which is
  "full-grown". In the case of people, it is the
  word for adults. It is used of both animals and
  humans, and is the opposite of children and
  youth. Adults capable of reproduction are
  "perfect" or full-grown. *Brethren, do not be*
  children in understanding; however, in malice
  be babes, but in understanding be mature (I
  Corinthians 14:20).

- It is used of completing a task. In Acts 20:24,
  Paul spoke about his desire *to "...finish my race*
  with joy, and the ministry which I received
  from the Lord Jesus, to testify to the gospel of
  the grace of God." Paul wanted to be faithful
  to God in fulfilling God's purpose for his life.

Jesus used the word in John 4:34 when He said He
wanted *"...to do the will of Him Who sent Me, and to finish*
His work." He used it again in John 17:4 when He said, *"I*
have finished the work which You have given Me to do."

Whatever "perfect" is, it is the same in nature or substance as that which is called "in part". The partial is a part of the perfect or the completed thing. That which is partial is described in verse 9 as being knowledge and prophecy. They refer to God's revelation. Should we not then conclude that "that which is perfect" is also referring to God's revelation?

The "perfect" thing that is coming is the completion of God's revelation to man. When it comes, the gifts that have given us new revelation from God are to be phased out. They were continually being phased out with the writing of each New Testament book. The process was completed with the writing of the final New Testament book.

This brings us to a crucial question: Is the Bible in its 66 books a complete and final revelation from God? My answer is an emphatic YES! The gift of tongues were to cease the moment this "perfect" thing was here. If the "perfect" thing is referring to the completion of the New Testament, then the biblical gift of tongues was to cease to exist at that point.

Is the Bible a Complete and Final Revelation from God?

How do we know that the Bible is a complete and final revelation from God? Jude 3 indicates that the point in time of God's revelation being spoken to man had already come:

Beloved, while I was very diligent to write to you concerning our common salvation, I found it necessary to write to you exhorting you to contend earnestly for the faith which was once for all delivered to the saints.

But how would we know that the last book in the process would be here? Would there always be a problem in church history of considering additional books? Should we be looking for that final book, or is it already here? The answer is found in the last book of the Bible:

I testify to everyone who hears the words of the prophecy of this book: If anyone adds to these things, God will add to him the plagues that are written in this book; and if anyone takes away from the words of the book of this prophecy, God shall take his part from the book of life, from the holy city, and from the things which are written in this book (Revelation 22:18-19).

Some argue that these verses are only to be applied to

the book of Revelation and not to the entire Bible. However, consider for a moment the contents of the book of Revelation. They deal with future events (at least from Chapter 4 on) all the way into the eternal state. How can you add anything to that? All that God will do in the future has been recorded. No one can add to it or take away from it without experiencing serious consequences!

Also, notice the argument of Hebrews 1:1,2:

God, Who at various times and in different ways
spoke in time past to the fathers by the prophets,
has in these last days spoken to us by His Son,
Whom He has appointed heir of all things,
through Whom also He made the worlds.

The Greek Text reads "in the last of these days". The "days" refer to the days of God's direct revelation by the prophets. In the last of these days in which God speaks directly, He will give final revelation about His Son, Jesus Christ.

The name of the last book of the New Testament is "The Revelation of Jesus Christ". Chapter 1 alone presents the resurrected Lord Jesus Christ in a way that was totally unknown in the Gospels. It is the final revelation of Jesus

Christ and explains all about His second coming and His
glory and majesty as our resurrected and exalted Lord.

The "perfect" thing that will come is the completed
Bible:

> *Be doers of the word, and not hearers only,*
> *deceiving yourselves. For if anyone is a hearer of*
> *the word and not a doer, he is like a man*
> *observing his natural face in a mirror; for he*
> *observes himself, goes away, and immediately*
> *forgets what kind of man he was. But he who*
> *looks into the perfect law of liberty and*
> *continues in it, and is not a forgetful hearer but*
> *a doer of the word, this one will be blessed in*
> *what he does* (James 1:22-25).

The use of the mirror as an illustration reminds us of I
Corinthians 13:12, which says, "For now we see in a
mirror". The word, "perfect" in James 1:25 is an adjective
modifying the word, "law", obviously referring to God's
Word. God's Word is complete. Psalm 119:89 reminds us,
"Forever, O Lord, Your word is settled in heaven." God's
revelation (as to its final and complete form communicated
to man) was settled long ago in heaven before it was ever
given to man. If God did not want to put a stamp of finality

on His written Word, He easily could have eliminated Revelation 22:18,19!

As wonderful as God's revelation is and as marvelous as the gifts for communicating it are (prophecy, knowledge, tongues), God's love is greater because it will never fail!

We are glad for everyone who discovers spiritual gifts and uses them for the glory of God and the building up of His church, but never forget that love is greater. Love is eternal, it never fails! Gifts are temporary regardless of your viewpoint as to how long they will be needed! In all your effort to discover your spiritual gifts, do not neglect God's love. It is even more important than using your gifts. Without God's love, your spiritual gifts are ineffective in the building up of every believer. God's love is what actually builds people up.

Things Don't Last Forever

Why do things not last forever? Because we grow up!

When I was a child, I spoke as a child, I understood as a child, I thought as a child; but when I became a man, I put away childish things (I Corinthians 13:11).

The words "put away" are the same as in verses 8 and 10. The "things" of the child refer to prophecies and knowledge, that which is "partial" and not "perfect" or "complete". They are lacking in complete understanding like the child (Greek *nepios* – "one without speech", used of toddlers).

God's love is the way of maturity. Knowledge, understanding, spiritual gifts, etc. can be reflective of immaturity especially when God's love is absent. The "perfect" thing (God's complete revelation) gives us understanding about God's love and God's ways that produce a mature, loving lifestyle. God's love never fails but spiritual gifts will run their course because they are temporary.

Some Bible teachers believe that the "perfect" thing is love itself. There is reason for this from John 4:18, where the word "perfect" is applied to the word "love"; however, the "perfect" thing in I Corinthians 13:10 had not arrived as yet (at least at the time of writing I Corinthians, 50–52 A.D.). Yet God's love was certainly available at that time!

Others insist that the "perfect" thing refers to Jesus Christ at His second coming. They are especially influenced by the phrase in I Corinthians 13:12, "face to face". Perhaps the words of an old Christian song affects this. The title of that old song is "Face to Face with Christ My Savior". But the adjective "perfect" in I Corinthians 13:10 is a neuter gender. If it were to be applied to Jesus Christ, it would need to be masculine.

Some believe that the word "perfect" applies to the event of Christ's second coming, or to the future millennial age or the eternal state. There is a lack of evidence for these views although we certainly have a right to state them as possible viewpoints.

A few have argued that the word, "perfect", applies to the universal body of Christ, the church. I Corinthians 12, the chapter which precedes the love chapter, certainly does refer to the principles of body life among church members. The spiritual gifts (in this view) would continue until the body of Christ is completed, obviously at the end of the church age when Jesus Christ returns for His church.

Some teach that the word, "perfect", refers to Paul's usage in Ephesians 4:13, where he says that all believers should "...come to the unity of the faith and the knowledge of the Son of God, to a perfect man, to the measure of the stature of the fullness of Christ." This view argues that "perfect" refers to Christian maturity and that seems to be supported by the illustration of I Corinthians 13:11, *"...when I became a man, I put away childish things"*. The problem is in determining whether that maturity is the maturity of the individual believers or of the corporate body of believers and if so, when can we say that "maturity" has come?

In spite of the good points favoring each of these views of the "perfect" thing, it still seems best and the most consistent view with other Scriptures to hold that the "perfect" refers to God's complete revelation in written form – namely, the Bible. Its obvious identification with the partial (prophecies and knowledge) seems to give strong support to this view. Also, the usage of the "mirror" in I Corinthians 13:12 is connected with other passages dealing with the Word of God (cf. I Corinthians 3:18; James 1:22-25). The word "perfect" is also used of God's Word in James 1:25.

The Problem of the Mirror

I Corinthians 13:12 states:

Now we see in a mirror, dimly, but then face to face. Now I know in part, but then I shall know just as I also am known.

The use of the word, "mirror", appears only here and in James 1:25. The word, "dimly", comes from a word that gives us our English word, "enigma". It means "...in obscurity".

Things are like riddles now, according to Paul. We don't see everything properly or correctly. Numbers 12:8 uses the Greek word translated, "dimly", in the Greek translation of the old Testament Hebrew (the Septuagint):

I speak with him face to face, even plainly and not in dark sayings; and he sees the form of the Lord. Why then were you not afraid to speak against My servant Moses?

The words, "dark sayings", use the same Greek word as in I Corinthians 13:12, translated, "dimly". The phrase ,"face to face", in Numbers 12:8 also appears in I Corinthians 13:12. The Lord said that He would make Himself known to Moses. There would be no obscurity in His communication with Moses. At the time Paul wrote I Corinthians, the knowledge they had was often "obscure". It was not completely clear.

Paul also wrote, "Now I know in part." The partial knowledge he had was tremendous in comparison to the

Corinthians, but Paul's knowledge was still not complete. It would be many years after his death that God would finally bring an end to His revelations to man (about 95 A.D., when John wrote the last book of the New Testament, The Revelation of Jesus Christ).

No matter what you know or do not know, without God's love you will not be effective in ministry to others. Today we have a complete written revelation from God to man for all of us to study. But the need for God's love is just as strong in our lives today as it was when Paul wrote I Corinthians. God's love will continue forever. There is always room to grow in understanding and experiencing the love of God.

The tendency of the Corinthians was to have spiritual pride because of their knowledge (cf. I Corinthians 8:1) and their spiritual gifts (I Corinthians 12). Paul's argument in chapter 13 is that the gifts were temporary and that their knowledge was incomplete. There was more coming than what they presently had available to them.

They were pursuing the wrong things – knowledge and spiritual gifts. I Corinthians 14:1 tells the Corinthians to "pursue love". Desiring (being enthusiastic or zealous for) spiritual gifts was fine, especially when they knew the importance of certain gifts (like prophecy), but God's love was the greatest thing of all since it never fails. Their present knowledge was incomplete and their usage of gifts would not last, but God's love was permanent and eternal!

One day a young man with a great desire to teach God's Word came into my office to talk with me. He had many talents and was a good student of God's Word. His ability to teach at his age was far superior to mine when I was his age. I marveled at his gift and his understanding.

But he had a problem – people were not responding to his teaching. He asked why, and I asked him, "Do you love the people you are teaching?" He was taken back by the question, and spent a few moments reflecting on it. Showing why he is going to be used of God in a great way, he said, "Thanks. I needed that reminder. Without love we are nothing." He was teachable.

We will not always know everything we would like to know, nor settle matters that we would like to settle. But we can always experience and exercise a little more of God's love. There are some things that we will never understand until we get to heaven! There are no doubt some things that we will never know about God even after we do get to heaven since His greatness is "past our finding out".

Two of the staff members who used to work for me were
not getting along. A particular issue that seemed minor to
others was very important to both of them. They were not
young men starting out in the ministry; both had years of
experience behind them. They saw this particular issue in
two different ways. Each felt he was right and the other was
wrong. Neither of them wanted to give in. Both assured me
that they loved each other, but that this issue had to be
settled.

The problem was that the issue was of such a nature
that a moral verdict as to who was right and who was
wrong was totally impossible. There was no chapter and
verse to which we could turn. Instead, I appealed to them
to love each other no matter what happened. They insisted
that they did love each other, but still would not give in.

It took quite a while to convince them from the Word
of God that "giving in" could be a demonstration of God's
love. The whole thing seemed bigger than what it really
was. But I once again saw that God was teaching them, and
myself, a little more about His love than any of us had
encountered before.

Future Understanding

Two things are said about the future understanding of the Corinthians, both preceded by the word, "then". The word, "then", is connected with the word, "when", in verse 10. When the perfect comes, then two things will happen:

• Then ... face to face

• Then ... I shall know just as I also am known

Some say that the "face-to-face" phrase could refer to being in heaven and seeing the Lord "face to face". Our knowledge when we see the Lord will certainly be superior to what it is now! However, this phrase could also be referring to the complete revelation of God in written form. Verse 10 says, *"When that which is perfect has come,"* and verse 12 completes it with, *"Then face to face."*

The phrase "face to face" should be connected with the word "mirror". "Face to face" is how we look into a "mirror". At the time of writing I Corinthians, things were not clear. They saw in the "mirror dimly". But when the entire New Testament would be completed, they would see clearly, or "face to face".

In Genesis 32:30, Jacob says, *"I have seen God face to face."* Yet the Bible says in John 1:18, *"No one has seen God at any time."* Jacob did have some direct knowledge about God, but he (as a mere man) could not see God or know all there is to know about Him. The finite cannot comprehend the infinite. In Judges 6:22 Gideon says, *"I have seen the Angel of the Lord face to face."* He was not convinced of that fact until he saw him perform a miracle in his presence. He saw before him what appeared to be a mere man, but his understanding greatly increased when he saw the miracle.

Perhaps the best explanation of the phrase, "face to face", is the one in Numbers 12:6-8:

If there is a prophet among you, I, the Lord, make Myself known to him in a vision, and I speak to him in a dream. Not so with My servant Moses; he is faithful in all My house. I speak with him face to face, even plainly, and not in dark sayings; and he sees the form of the Lord. Why then were you not afraid to speak against My servant Moses?

The knowledge and understanding of Moses is being contrasted with the knowledge of other prophets to whom God would speak. This text seems to be the one Paul might have had in mind when he was writing I Corinthians 13:12.

The phrase, *"Then I shall know just as I also am known"*, could refer to being in heaven with the Lord, but more likely it refers to God's complete revelation in written form. A complete, full understanding of the plan of God is found in the Bible. It was not complete when I Corinthians was written, but by the end of the first century A.D. it was. The words, *"just as I also am known"*, refer to God's knowledge of him in terms of his salvation.

Paul's knowledge would be brought up to that particular level of understanding when the Word of God was completed. Naturally, there will be much more to learn in eternity!

Even those who believe that this full knowledge is not the written Bible but future heavenly knowledge, will admit that we will continue to learn and to know things forever and ever!

Though several viewpoints have been given on these verses, one thing remains clear to all: God's love will not fail! Certain gifts will no longer be needed. Things don't last forever. God's love will still be there and still needed. Our greatest need is still God's love, and it always will be!

Love Is the Greatest

Now abide faith, hope, love, these three; but the
greatest of these is love.

God's love is greater than all the spiritual gifts that the
Holy Spirit has given to the believers. It is greater in future
endurance and it is also greater in present experience.
God's love is now.

The words, *"And now abide..."* are present tense in
Greek. This means that God's love constantly, continually
abides. Along with love, two other things continue to abide
– faith and hope; but love is the greatest of the three!

When my oldest son was just a little boy, I invited him
to jump off our backyard fence into my arms. He hesitated
and said he was afraid. I said, "Don't you believe that Daddy
can catch you?" He said he believed me. I think he hoped I
would make good on my promise, even though he
suspected the possibility of error!

Finally I said, "Do you believe that Dad loves you very
much?" At that point he jumped! Fortunately, I caught him.
My love for him persuaded him to trust me. Faith and hope
are important, but love is greater and stronger.

My faith in the Lord is questionable at times, but His love for me never is! My hope in Him is shaky at times, but I am absolutely secure in His love. Salvation is not based upon my ability to believe; it is based on a loving God who loves me even though He knows what I am like. His love has granted me total forgiveness because of what His Son did for me at the cross. John 3:16 puts it so beautifully:

For God so loved the world that He gave His only begotten Son, that whoever believes in Him should not perish but have everlasting life.

The strength and security of God's love is wonderfully portrayed in the Song of Solomon as Solomon expresses his love for his one and only, a woman named Abishag. Abishag tenderly speaks of the strength and security of Solomon's love for her:

Set me as a seal upon your heart, as a seal upon your arm; for love is as strong as death, jealousy as cruel as the grave; its flames are flames of fire, a most vehement flame. Many waters cannot quench love, nor can the floods drown it. If a man would give for love all the wealth of his house, it would be utterly despised (Song of Solomon 8:6,7).

The Lord reminded the nation of Israel of His faithful and unconditional love for them. He said through Moses:

You are a holy people to the Lord your God; the Lord your God has chosen you to be a people for Himself, a special treasure above all the peoples on the face of the earth. The Lord did not set His love on you or choose you because you were more in number than any other people, for you were the least of all peoples; but because the Lord loves you, and because He would keep the oath which He swore to your fathers, the Lord has brought you out with a mighty hand, and redeemed you from the house of bondage, from the hand of Pharaoh king of Egypt. Therefore know that the Lord your God, He is God, the faithful God who keeps covenant and mercy for a thousand generations with those who love Him and keep His commandments (Deuteronomy 7:6-9).*

It is God's faithful love that brings security to the believer. It removes all doubts, it strengthens our faith; it encourages our hope and trust in His promises. It is because of His love for us that we have any degree of confidence. This point is made clear:

*Love has been perfected among us in this; that
we may have boldness in the day of judgment;
because as He is, so are we in this world. There
is no fear in love; but perfect love casts out fear,
because fear involves torment. But he who fears
has not been made perfect in love. We love Him
because He first loved us* (I John 4:17-19).

We cannot explain our salvation on the basis of our
personal worthiness or dedicated efforts to do what is right.
We cannot earn, nor do we deserve our salvation from sin,
death and hell. There is only one explanation – "God so
loved the world! " Ephesians 2:4 says, *"But God, who is rich
in mercy, because of His great love with which He loved us
...."*

Paul reminds us of the greatness and security of God's
love:

*I am persuaded that neither death nor life, nor
angels nor principalities nor powers, nor things
present nor things to come, nor height nor
depth, nor any other created thing, shall
separate us from the love of God which is in
Christ Jesus our Lord* (Romans 8:38,39).

Nothing can ever separate us from God's love! What a wonderful confidence, what blessed assurance! No angel or demon from hell can ever separate us! No king, ruler or authority of any kind can remove us from the security of God's love! Events and circumstances, whether past or present, cannot separate us! Praise God!

What Do Faith, Hope and Love Have in Common?

A fascinating little problem is found in the Greek text of I Corinthians 13:13. The word, "abide", is in the singular form rather than the plural. One would expect the plural since three things are mentioned that abide - faith, hope and love.

One possible solution is that the writer expects the reader to supply the word "abide" after each of the three qualities in that verse. Faith abides, hope abides and love abides. However, the phrase that ends the first statement, "these three", seems to point to a relationship between the three qualities rather than viewing them separately.

The writer seems to suggest that all three belong together. They have something in common. They are treated as one. It is only one thing that continues to abide, and it is best described by three words - faith, hope and love.

These three qualities are seen together in several passages in the New Testament. In Romans 5:1-5 faith is mentioned in verses 1 and 2, hope in verses 4 and 5 and love in verse 5. In Colossians 1:4,5 we find all three together:

*Since we heard of your **faith** in Christ Jesus and of your **love** for all the saints; because of the **hope** which is laid up for you in heaven, of which you heard before in the word of the truth of the gospel.*

In Ephesians 1:15-18 we have faith and love in verse 15, and hope in verse 18. 1 Thessalonians 1:3 puts them all together again:

*Remembering without ceasing your work of **faith**, labor of **love**, and patience of **hope** in our Lord Jesus Christ in the sight of our God and Father.*

Out of all the gifts, attributes and resources available to the believer, nothing so characterizes what is really important and eternal as do those three words: faith, hope and love. Every other attribute, attitude and action somehow flows out of those three. Those three qualities describe the total of what God wants for us and has for us.

Everything seems simple and clear when described by these three words. They can only flow out of a regenerated heart, one that has received a new nature from God. In man's natural state, he does not have these three qualities flowing out of his life. Only God can give us faith, hope and love!

Consider the following things which faith, hope and love have in common:

- All three are the result of God's work in the heart of the believer.

Apart from divine intervention, man is incapable of experiencing either faith, hope or love. Man is described as being "dead in trespasses and sins" (Ephesians 2:1). Being spiritually dead, he is unable to respond with faith, hope or love. He must be born again by the Spirit of God. Only then can he have true faith, hope and love. Faith and love are stated to be "fruit" of the Holy Spirit in Galatians 5:22,23, and in that text, the word "hope" could be inserted as part of what joy, peace and patience are all about.

- All three describe the maturity which God desires in the life of every believer.

The Corinthians were immature (I Corinthians 14:20) and carnal (I Corinthians 3:3). Their spiritual pride kept them from discovering true maturity in the Lord (as it does to many people today). Faith, hope and love were better qualities than what they were manifesting in their lives. If you want to describe spiritual maturity from God's viewpoint, then use God's words – faith, hope and love. They tell it all. Nothing is left out!

•   All three are eternal and will be found in
    heaven as well as on earth.

Some have tried to show the greatness of love over faith and hope by saying that faith and hope will no longer be needed when we get to heaven. They say, "Faith will be turned to sight and hope will finally be realized. Heaven appears to be the end of faith and hope as far as the believer is concerned."

But the Bible does not teach that. It is true that II Corinthians 5:7 says, *"For we walk by faith, not by sight."* But this does not mean that we will not need faith when we get to heaven. On the contrary, Hebrews 11:6 says,

"Without faith it is impossible to please Him, for he who comes to God must believe that He is,

and that He is a rewarder of those who diligently
seek Him."

There will be more reasons in heaven to have faith in
God than we have now! Dependency and trust upon our
living God will be greater then than now!

Heaven will be a wonderful place as we continue to
discover and learn more and more about our wonderful
Lord. Our faith will grow as our knowledge of Him
increases, just like it does now. We will not be sitting upon
clouds doing nothing; heaven is not the end, but only the
beginning of faith!

Hope is the anticipation of things promised. In heaven,
hope will become more exciting. Realization and
anticipation of God's promises and blessings will be lifted to
new heights. We will not automatically see and know
everything there is to know when we get to heaven. We will
continue to learn and grow in our understanding and
experience. Our hope will expand as we realize the infinite
resources and possibilities we have available to us because
an infinite God can make them possible. Revelation 21:5
says, *"Behold, I make all things new."* Praise God!

Just as love continues to grow on earth, so it will

increase continually in heaven. I John 4:7,8 tells us that love is from God and that *"God is love"*. Since God is infinite, it is obvious that the depth of love will never be discovered! We will continue to learn about God's love.

Oh, the depth of the riches both of the wisdom and knowledge of God! How unsearchable are His judgments and His ways past finding out! (Romans 11:33).

When you "fall in love" with another person here on earth, that love fluctuates from day to day as you experience a multitude of attitudes, reactions and circumstances that affect your love. God's love, which is not based on a moment's pleasure or an emotional feeling, continues to grow as the relationship deepens and all of life is shared with the person you love. Love definitely grows. It becomes stronger and more reliable. It treasures, honors and delights in the object of its affections and expands in its appreciation of the other person's qualities. Love cares, responds, creates, sustains, encourages and touches all aspects of another person's life and as a result, it deepens through the years.

Love in heaven will continue. God's inexhaustible resources make His love a continual discovery and blessing. Throughout eternity, we will experience the depth and dimensions of the love of God.

That in ages to come He might show the exceeding riches of His grace in His kindness toward us in Christ Jesus (Ephesians 2:7).

Why Is Love Greater Than Faith and Hope?

Faith, hope and love are present in our lives now, and will be throughout eternity. But the interesting and featured point of I Corinthians 13:13 is the statement:

But the greatest of these is love.

Why is that so? Faith and hope are certainly great and very needed. Why is love more important? What can it do that faith and hope cannot?

I Corinthians 14:1 begins with the words, "Pursue love" and, in the light of the last statement of chapter 13, we can easily see why. If love is the greatest, then it should be a major priority in our lives. We ought to go after it with all our energies. We must give time to this pursuit and determine to have God's love above all else! Is that what you understand to be your greatest need? And if so, what are you going to do about it?

Are your priorities at the present time reflecting your

pursuit of love? What time have you given today to cultivating this most important quality in your life? Is it really "number one" with you? Do you really want it more than you want financial reward or success? Do you really prefer God's love to personal pleasure?

Consider the following reasons why love is the greatest.

- Love is greater than faith and hope because God is love.

God is not merely love, for He is that plus much more. It is not correct to say, "Love is God" for that makes God an emotion and brings Him down to a human level. God is loving, but that doesn't say it all either. I John 4:8 says, *"God is love."* The essence of His being and character, the motivation of His acts, the basis of His relationship to us is love.

His love does not exclude His holiness or His righteousness. His love does not overlook or excuse sin. His love does not eliminate judgment or hell. His love is perfect in every way and very different from the natural tendency of man and woman.

The Bible does not say, "God is faith" or, "God is hope".

He **gives** us faith and hope, but it is only of love that the Bible declares, "God is ...." Therefore, love is greater than faith and hope because it is the very nature and character of God himself.

- Love is greater than faith and hope because without God's love, we would have no faith or hope.

Faith and hope in our hearts are put there by the love of God. It is God's love that is the ground upon which faith and hope are built. They, in turn, direct our hearts to love God Who first loved us (I John 4:19).

John 3:16 says, *"For God so loved the world."* That's where it starts. Jesus Christ came because of the Father's love.

In this the love of God was manifested toward us, that God has sent His only begotten Son into the world, that we might live through Him. In this is love, not that we loved God, but that He loved us and sent His Son to be the propitiation for our sins (I John 4:9,10).

Jesus Christ died on the cross for our sins because of His great love.

God demonstrates His own love toward us, in
that while we were still sinners, Christ died for
us (Romans 5:8).

By this we know love, because He laid down His
life for us (I John 3:16).

We are saved because of God's great love. Ephesians 2:4
states that God's mercy toward us in salvation *is "...because*
of His great love for us". Without God's love, there would be
no faith and hope. His love has made it all possible. We
believe in Him because He loves us; we have hope in Him
because of His love for us.

- Love is greater than faith and hope because of
  its wider application.

Faith and hope are both directed toward God alone.
Love is not only directed to God (although that is the first
priority) but also to others, both believers and nonbelievers.
According to the Bible, the more love we have toward God,
the greater will be the love we have toward others.

Whoever has this world's goods, and sees his
brother in need, and shuts up his heart from
him, how does the love of God abide in him?

Little children, let us not love in word or in tongue, but in deed and truth (I John 3:17,18).

If God's love is controlling our hearts and actions, it will show in our care and concern for others.

Beloved, if God so loved us, we also ought to love one another (I John 4:11).

If someone says, "I love God" and hates his brother, he is a liar, for he who does not love his brother whom he has seen, how can he love God Whom he has not seen? And this commandment we have from Him: that he who loves God must love his brother also (John 4:20,21).

Faith is centered in God alone; hope is based on what God has said and its object is God's Word. The Bible warns us to not put faith in man or hope in this life, but love is different. We are not only to love God, but also to love others. Love has a wider application.

• Love is greater than faith and hope because it is the primary motive for obedience and service.

The apostle Paul wrote in II Corinthians 5:14 that *"...the love of Christ constrains us."* The love of Jesus Christ for us is the driving force behind all Christian commitment and ministry. In John 14:15, Jesus said, *"If you love Me, keep My commandments."* God's love is not controlling a rebellious and disobedient life. When we decide to violate God's commands, we indicate our lack of love for God.

> *By this we know that we love the children of God, when we love God and keep His commandments. For this is the love of God, that we keep His commandments. And His commandments are not burdensome* (I John 5:2,3).

If we love God, we will obey Him. That principle is evident in our homes and families. The natural response of our children is to disobey. Rules and regulations that we impose upon them do not remove the desire to disobey; they only heighten and intensify that desire. Paul spoke of that problem:

> *Sin, taking opportunity by the commandment, produced in me all manner of evil desire. For apart from the law sin was dead. I was alive once without the law, but when the commandment came, sin revived and I died* (Romans 7:8,9).

Paul said in I Timothy 1:9 that the law was not made for a righteous man but for those who are lawless and rebellious. Obedience to God's commands cannot be controlled by man or his laws; the motivation to obey arises out of God's love. Loving God produces a submissive heart, a willingness to obey. It is hard at times to admit that the reason we do not obey God is because we do not love God!

- Love is greater than faith and hope because love is that which edifies other believers.

Ephesians 4:15 tells us to speak the truth in love. In verse 16, we read that true believers are built up in the sphere or arena of love. I Corinthians 8:1 tells us that love edifies.

I need to grow in my faith and my hope in the Lord. That benefits me and perhaps indirectly affects others by way of my example. But that which builds up other believers is love! Colossians 3:12-14 speaks powerfully to this point:

As the elect of God, holy and beloved, put on tender mercies, kindness, humbleness of mind, meekness, longsuffering, bearing with one another, and forgiving one another, if anyone has a complaint against another; even as Christ forgave you, so you also must do. But above all these things put on love, which is the bond of perfection.

Above everything else, we need love! Believers will experience their unity through the application of God's love. Galatians 5:13 exhorts us to serve one another through love.

- Love is greater than faith and hope because love can do what faith and hope cannot do.

Faith does not forgive, and neither does hope, but love does. Ephesians 4:32-5:2 tells us to forgive one another, and that this is possible if we learn to walk in love as Jesus Christ has loved us:

Be kind to one another, tenderhearted, forgiving one another, just as God in Christ also forgave you. Therefore be followers of God as dear children. And walk in love, as Christ also has loved us and given Himself for us, an offering and a sacrifice to God for a sweet-smelling aroma.

It is the love of Jesus Christ that has forgiven us of our sins. We deserve judgment and hell. Thank God for His great love! I Peter 4:8 says that *"...love will cover a multitude of sins."*

A marriage cannot be what God wants it to be without God's love and continually forgiving each other. There have been many times when I have failed to live up to the expectations of my wife, children and others. I have disappointed them both in what I have done and what I have not done. Thank God for forgiveness – without it our marriages and families would have difficulty surviving!

- Love is greater than faith and hope because it does not depend upon things outside itself in order to function.

Faith requires an object to be trusted. Romans 10:17 says, *"So then faith comes by hearing, and hearing by the word of God."* Our faith does not save us; Jesus Christ saves us! Our faith rests upon Jesus Christ as we learn of Him in the Bible.

Hope is based on promises. God promises things to us that we have yet to experience. Romans 8:24,25 tells us about the importance of hope:

We were saved in this hope, but hope that is seen
is not hope; for why does one still hope for what
he sees? But if we hope for what we do not see,
then we eagerly wait for it with perseverance.

Our hope is not "whistling in the dark" but is rather "an anchor of the soul" (Hebrews 6:19), a hope "both sure and steadfast". The reason for this is the character of God Himself: It is because God cannot lie (Hebrews 6:18) that we have hope. What God promises, He will perform. Our hope is strong because of who God is.

God's love, in contrast to faith and hope, does not require a response or a reason in order to exist and function. Human love demands a response: "If you love me, then I'll love you." But God's love is different. Even when people do not respond and are quite antagonistic to you, you can still love them with God's love.

Love is greater than faith and hope in that love toward others works even when there is no reason or response. God's love continues to give and give, without thought of what it receives in return. The joy of giving dominates the one who knows God's love. The world says, "Grab all the gusto you can get!" It continually reminds us to "...get it while you can", but that's not the way God's love responds. It gives!

I had the joy a few years ago of sharing with a friend that God's love is really the greatest thing of all, and definitely the greatest need in his life. He and his wife were going through some difficult times. His wife became very discouraged and started to withdraw from church activities and social occasions. She wondered about God's love for her because of the things that had happened in her life. They are both Christians, and he often referred to her problems, seeking help for her.

On this particular day, I was able to share with him in a special way what rarely happens between two men. He was quite sensitive and tears filled his eyes. He really wanted help, and that's where it starts: You must want help. I told him that the reason his wife was insecure and discouraged was his problem, not hers. She needed a husband who would love her for who she was, including all her problems.

He was very demanding as a person, and I told him that day that he needed to stop expecting things of her. He wanted her to change so badly and was not accepting her like she was. He was self-centered in his goals and interests. He was a strong leader, and active in serving the Lord.

He did not seem to understand that love surpasses

knowledge, and that knowledge makes you arrogant. He loves to study and can comment on almost any subject. He is well-read and communicates with others easily.

But he needed to be broken inside for he was proud of what he knew and of his ability to handle things. One exception which was devastating him was his ability to handle his wife. We spoke long about the love of God. As we talked, I could see him change in his viewpoints. If he would start loving his wife with God's love, stop all expectations and demands and accept her unconditionally, she would become more secure, gain new confidence and become a blessing to her husband and to others.

The good news for this couple is that God's love did exactly what it promised to do. They are now serving the Lord together and are very happy in their relationship with each other.

This story is repeated over and over in the lives of people. The greatest need we all have (once we become believers in Jesus Christ) is to be controlled by God's great love. His love is truly the greatest! The Holy Spirit of God produces that love in the heart of the Spirit-filled believer. Knowing about love is important, but when it's working on your life, it surpasses knowledge (Ephesians 3:19).

Love and Priorities

The application of God's love in our lives is where we usually have difficulty. We should learn about God's love and a study of I Corinthians 13 is a good place to start, but it can't stop with knowing about it; we have to apply it.

This study convinced me that simply knowing about God's love is not enough. I have spent many hours studying this subject and reading the books of others, but this does not mean that I am experiencing it. I was keenly aware of that fact during the hours of preparing this study. I was sharing with a friend about what I was learning and, at the same time, getting upset by a lack of response to my great revelations! I felt the Spirit of God's convicting power as I realized my failure to reflect the very love about which I was writing!

Many people spell "love" with the word "time". Love is interpreted in terms of the amount of time that is given. Time is a matter of priorities. We usually give time to that which is important to us. Sometimes it is embarrassing to take a good long look at how we spend our time. We waste much of it and yet, in a certain sense, we are doing what we want with it. Our priorities are not always right but when something is important to us, we usually take the time to do it.

Believers are exhorted to love God first and foremost, above everything and everyone else. Jesus Christ made this quite clear:

You shall love the Lord your God with all your heart, with all your soul, and with all your mind. This is the first and great commandment. And the second is like it: You shall love your neighbor as yourself. On these two commandments hang all the Law and the Prophets (Matthew 22:37-40).

The first priority is God Himself. The second priority is "your neighbor" ... others. Jesus Christ said that the world would know that we are His disciples if we love one another (John 13:34,35). He called this the "new commandment". Loving other believers is not an option, but a command.

One day, a friend was telling me of all he was doing to share his faith in Jesus Christ. He had the best methods and what he felt was the "right approach". He spent many hours at it and he seemed proud of his accomplishments. I was struck by his absence of love for other believers, however, in his conversation. He was caustic and critical of other believers, often putting them down for not doing things the way he was doing them.

I confronted him with the words of the Bible about love for one another, but he didn't respond. I felt sorry for him. Today, he does not have an effective ministry. He is bitter and still has problems loving others. Little does he realize that loving other believers would enhance his witness to nonbelievers. When they see our love for one another, then they will become convinced that we are the disciples of Jesus Christ!

Sixteen times in the New Testament we are told to *"...love one another"*. On two of those occasions, we are exhorted to love one another *"fervently"* (I Peter 1:22; 4:8). To love one another the way God wants us to takes some hard work!

The Key to Experiencing God's Love

For one thing, we need to become believers in Jesus Christ in order to experience and enjoy God's wonderful love. I John 4:19 says, *"We love Him because He first loved us."* The word "Him" is not in the Greek text. It simply says, *"We love ... because He first loved us,"* - our **capacity** to love is rooted in His love for us.

God's love is the fruit, the product of the Holy Spirit's

work in the believer (Galatians 5:22). All believers have the Holy Spirit dwelling in them (I Corinthians 6:19), but just because you have the Holy Spirit of God within you does not mean that the Holy Spirit of God is controlling you and producing God's love in your life.

Sin grieves (Ephesians 4:30) and quenches (I Thessalonians 5:19) the Holy Spirit of God. Sinful lifestyles and practices resist the work of the Spirit (I Thessalonians 4:3-8), and until we confess our sin and repent (forsake it; turn from it; stop doing it), the flow of God's love through us will be hindered. Galatians 5:16 says that if we walk in the Spirit, we will not carry out the lust of the flesh. A real battle is going on inside of us between our sinful desires and the Holy Spirit. To walk in the Spirit is to be obedient to what the Spirit has revealed in the Word of God, the Bible.

Spiritual love enhances all other forms of love. Sexual love must be controlled by spiritual love or it will violate God's Word and hurt the lives of others. Friendship love must be controlled by spiritual love or our relationships with others will become empty, hurtful and unproductive. Family love must be controlled by spiritual love or we will isolate ourselves, trying to walk alone and be independent; we will lack a sense of belonging that is filled with loving care and provision of needs.

God's love is the greatest thing in all the world, and it is produced by God's Holy Spirit in the life of true believers in Jesus Christ.

In every area of our lives, our greatest need is love!